Thought Leaders

Essays from innovators

Edited by Pravin Raj, Syed Hoda,
and Howard Lock

Connected Transportation

The Cisco Systems® Internet Business Solutions Group (IBSG) is a global consulting team that helps customers transform their organizations by strategically applying advanced technologies and business process innovation. A unique combination of industry experience, business, and technical knowledge enables IBSG consultants to serve as trusted advisors to many of the world's top organizations.

Serving as a catalyst for change, the Cisco Systems® IBSG Transportation team works with leading transportation businesses and authorities worldwide. This team is responsible for leading Cisco's customer partnerships, helping organizations turn their technology investments into strategic assets that increase productivity, reduce costs, and create new revenue sources. Senior transportation industry executives find immense value in having access to Cisco IBSG's Internet knowledge base, best practices, and proven, benchmarked results.

CISCO SYSTEMS

Published by
Torworth Publishing
35 The Strand
Walmer
Kent CT14 7DX
lesley.daley@torworth.org

First published 2006

ISBN 0-9551959-0-X

Special thanks to the executive sponsors:
Gary Bridge, Toby Burton, and Mohsen Moazami

Thank you to: David Critchley, Lothar Geuenich, Anna Lin, Judy May, John Morrell, Eugene Tay, and Dr. Curt Tompkins

Edited by Pravin Raj, Syed Hoda, and Howard Lock
Design by Loman Street Studio
Cover images by Getty Images
Printed by G&B Printers

A catalogue record for this book is available from the British Library.

Contents

Contents

Contributing Editors
The following people at the Cisco Systems
Internet Business Solutions Group (IBSG)
have also been responsible for the editorial
content of Connected Transportation:

Gerald Charles, Jr. I Director, Public Sector, IBSG
Dr. Amir Fattah I Senior Executive Advisor, IBSG
Valentin Stoyanov I Director, IBSG

Introduction

Meeting global transportation demand through increased infrastructure utilization

Pravin Raj I Director, Global Transportation Lead, Cisco Systems IBSG
Syed Hoda I Director, Retail and Transportation, Cisco Systems IBSG
Howard Lock I Senior Executive Advisor, Transportation, Cisco Systems IBSG

From Nile River trade routes and the famed Silk Road to the jet airplanes and bullet trains of the modern era, transportation systems have evolved dramatically as civilizations—and entire economies—have met the challenge to get themselves, and their goods, from origin to destination faster and with increased efficiency.

Today, despite its astonishing technological and organizational underpinnings, the U.S.$3 trillion transportation industry faces a major crisis. Global demand is growing at an unprecedented rate. "Our biggest challenges by far are the joint problems of growing demand and infrastructure lag," says David Neeleman, CEO of JetBlue Airways.

In trying to meet this demand, the laws of physics, constraints on available space, and public tolerance for infrastructure have, in most cases, been pushed to the limit. The executives and public officials managing our transportation systems simply cannot expand supply or throttle back demand. The solution is to find better ways to increase capacity *without* building new infrastructure.

This book contains essays from leaders of many of the largest and most influential transportation companies in the world, as well as from government policy-makers who both regulate and fund our transportation systems. Our authors often agree on the issues, but differ in their solutions. Their debates about how to obtain benefit from maturing technologies; how to implement business-process change; and how the public sector should intervene all require new thinking. Without some of the fresh approaches they propose, our existing transportation infrastructure may not support the next wave of global growth.

The global transportation industry at a crossroads

Historically, the transportation industry has met increased demand in one of two ways: (1) innovation in propulsion technologies, such as increased speed, or (2) expansion of physical infrastructure. The laws of physics, however, have caused train speeds to plateau at 180 miles per hour and air travel to hit Mach 0.8 for the last 40 years. In addition, automobiles cannot be driven safely at speeds much faster than they are today.

We have also reached the limits of both physical infrastructure and society's ability—or willingness—to pay for it. While capacity investment may be

relevant for India, China, and other developing countries, which have not yet reached infrastructure thresholds, this strategy has a limited role in the developed world. Real estate for road and port expansion is scarce and expensive, and environmental concerns are more critical than ever before. Most important, the sheer length of time it takes to design, approve, and construct a major infrastructure project means that demand growth will outstrip the capacity gains by the time the project is completed. Bill DeCota, Director of Aviation at the Port Authority of New York and New Jersey, puts it plainly: "What is clear is that many of the old solutions are no longer applicable. It used to be the case that if you ran out of space, you built a new terminal. That no longer works."

Today, despite its astonishing technological and organizational underpinnings, the U.S.$3 trillion transportation industry faces a major crisis.

Recently, some industry leaders have successfully implemented demand modulation strategies to balance capacity and demand more effectively. This approach involves managing demand via pricing mechanisms such as higher tolls, taxes, or fares; congestion pricing; and high-occupancy vehicle (HOV) lanes. Dr. Joseph Sussman, J.R. East Professor at Massachusetts Institute of Technology, is a proponent of this approach. He writes in his essay that the capacity of facilities (such as highways) remains fixed until they are either upgraded or replaced, and that capacity needs to be managed. "Core to that management is the notion of providing an incentive to use the facility outside peak times," Sussman says. "You spread demand, moving people onto the shoulders of the peaks using pricing, charging them differently at different times of day." Jeffrey Shane, Under Secretary for Policy at the U.S. Department of Transportation, takes a similar stance. "The use of tolls, congestion pricing, and user fees," he writes, "holds promise for helping to solve congestion and mobility problems and providing new revenues for infrastructure improvements."

But demand modulation is not feasible as an across-the-board strategy because it infringes on what is often viewed as a basic human right. So, what should the transportation industry do to meet demand that is already overwhelming existing infrastructure?

A new approach to increasing capacity

If we cannot travel faster, build enough infrastructure, or use demand pricing to meet this challenge, we must make better use of existing infrastructure. We believe that this approach is singularly suited to address the supply-demand imbalance. In order to increase capacity, we must simultaneously address productivity in all three facets of a transportation system—the infrastructure or fixed assets, the mobile assets, and the workforce.

Thanks to maturing technologies, capacity can be expanded quickly and at a significantly lower cost than building new infrastructure, thus delivering the greatest ROI for the industry.

Until now, the industry has focused on improving the utilization of each of these components in silos, resulting in sub-optimal impact and return on investment (ROI). For example, traffic-light synchronization improves traffic flow but is independent of the actual number of vehicles waiting at the light. Similarly, vehicle navigation systems help drivers navigate an urban environment, but they do not account for traffic accidents, congestion, or roadway repairs ahead.

Thanks to maturing technologies, capacity can be expanded quickly and at a significantly lower cost than building new infrastructure, thus delivering the greatest ROI for the industry.

Applying maturing technologies to increase capacity

High-speed wireless connectivity to the vehicle, remote sensing capabilities, and increased computing and storage capacities are some of the maturing technologies that enable increased capacity. Together, these technologies add intelligence at the point of service delivery—on the airplane, ship, train, or motor vehicle—resulting in greater interactions among the mobile assets themselves, and among the mobile assets and the central command center. These real-time interactions, in turn, drive greater productivity across the entire industry.

François Lamoureux, Director General of Transportation and Energy at the European Commission, holds a similar view. "The key," Lamoureux writes, "is the aggressive use of technologies that allow greater traffic management in an environment of growing demand for mobility. Technology is the key to optimizing usage of existing infrastructure capacity, and to harmonizing systems across the EU."

So what does a transportation system that uses technology to increase capacity look like? First, the system must sense the status of the infrastructure and the mobile assets that use it—for example, the highway and the automobile, the airspace and the aircraft, and the track and the train—and have an improved awareness of the demand on that infrastructure. The system must also quickly *analyze* the data it has sensed and interpret events based on predictive and adaptive models governed by business rules. And finally, it must respond quickly and appropriately to the data it has received and analyzed. In short, the system must include and fully integrate event-based processes, pervasive intelligence, and ubiquitous connectivity. Information sensed by one part of the transportation system can then be transmitted automatically to other parts of the system to trigger the appropriate response.

Real-world examples of the value of technology in increasing capacity—in all modes of transportation—abound. For example, forewarning drivers through wireless feeds about a highway accident could provide a wider range of route options and cut congestion. The same information, sent to the fire and police departments, could shorten the arrival time for emergency vehicles, alleviating traffic jams and possibly saving lives.

Or, take the example of an airplane that develops a problem in flight and must be removed from service. If the airplane incorporated sensors to relay diagnostics and parts information to maintenance prior to arrival, an engineer armed with the correct parts and tools could repair the plane as soon as it landed. The plane could then return to service sooner, reducing both airline cost and passenger inconvenience, and improving workforce productivity.

August Henningsen, CEO and Chairman of the Executive Board at Lufthansa Technik, explains the motivation for airlines to pursue a capacity-optimization strategy through technology. "[A]irlines simply cannot afford to have expensive aircraft sitting on the tarmac any longer than they have to," Henningsen writes, "and when you have 500 passengers onboard, you cannot keep them waiting while you decide how to tackle a maintenance issue. Only with the ongoing developments in technology are we going to be able to achieve even greater reliability and safety standards with increased visibility of information and increased integration of all aspects of the business."

Another example of the potentially positive impact of technology on the airline industry is "free flight." Sometimes referred to as the "Single Sky" initiative, free flight enables an aircraft to fly a flexible track across the sky instead of the fixed track currently mandated by air traffic control. This is made possible by advanced communications and global positioning systems that together enable aircraft to negotiate flight paths with air traffic managers and other aircraft in the operating air space—increasing aircraft productivity and airspace utilization.

"The physics are not going to change with regard to aircraft technology," writes Bill DeCota. "Planes are still going to land on the ground and people will still be going to a boarding gate 20 or 30 years from now. But while the air space itself is still finite, we can make much more efficient use of it."

Similarly, rail systems are eager to optimize existing physical infrastructure while reducing operating costs. *Air Cargo World*, a leading transportation publication, reported in October 2004 that "a reduction of one mile per hour in average train velocity creates an artificial need for another 250 to 300 railcars." One solution that increases capacity is Positive Train Control (PTC). Today, most types of train control use block signaling, which prevents a train from entering a block without explicit clearance. While this ensures safety of the people and assets, trains are forced to maintain a slower speed while awaiting clearance. In the near future, technology that follows the exact locations of trains will automatically prevent them from entering a block unless authorized. This approach constantly evaluates train movements to determine if intervention is necessary. As a result, trains are able to maintain a higher average speed, resulting in greater utilization of track capacity—and increased profits.

Improved profit margins are increasingly valuable at a time when physical transportation itself is becoming a commodity. "As our industry becomes increasingly commoditized," writes John Mullen, Joint Chief Executive of DHL Express and Management Board Member of Deutsche Post World Net, "we would rather add value than cut prices, so technology will beat the heart of innovations that enable us to make those differentiations."

Consumer benefits

It is not just transportation companies that benefit from these maturing technologies: consumers benefit as well. Every day consumers check real-time information on flight arrivals or departures using airline Websites, shipment status using cargo portals, and traffic congestion using highway Webcams. According to André Navarri, President of rail equipment manufacturer Bombardier Transportation, customer-centric train operators who can keep their passengers "connected" will give trains an advantage over cars. He sees the next step as installing on-train Wi-Fi along with Global System for Mobile Communications cabling to allow continuous mobile coverage, even in tunnels. "Experience shows that passengers will often wait until the next train if they know that it is more modern and offers them a more comfortable journey. So we know this kind of service makes passengers happy and can increase passenger numbers."

Looking further into the future, it is not hard to imagine how technology could make traveling easier. Suppose you are booked on a flight that is scheduled to depart at 6 p.m. The flight is scheduled on your calendaring software—as is a meeting away from your office at 3 p.m. Your calendaring software automatically checks with an online map service to find the optimal route to the airport and determines the current traffic and travel time for that route. If there has been a traffic accident, the software calculates the extra time the drive will now take, sends you a message—using Short Message Service (SMS) on your mobile handheld, for example—that warns you to leave now, and provides a listing of later flights with an option to rebook.

For most industries, radical transformation of business processes is required to realize the benefits of technology—both within the enterprise and throughout the value chain of suppliers, partners, and customers. The transportation industry is no different.

The examples given here are not wild fantasies. John Belcher, Chairman and CEO of ARINC, writes in his essay: "In many cases, the technology already exists to tackle these problems." He then cites broadband digital links, automatic vehicle location systems, and pico cell technology, which enables airborne cell phone calls, as examples of capabilities that have been around for years. But technology alone cannot ensure increased use of capacity. Two additional prerequisites exist. First, the industry must embrace process innovation by rethinking and reengineering entrenched business processes to make them more customer-centric. Second, industry must renegotiate the role of government in transportation, redefining the parameters of institutional collaboration.

Embracing process innovation

For most industries, radical transformation of business processes is required to realize the benefits of technology—both within the enterprise and throughout the value chain of suppliers, partners, and customers. The transportation industry is no different.

Today, transportation companies operate in silos, with disparate, mostly nonintegrated functional departments. For example, a typical airline has independent functional units handling reservations, ticketing, boarding, in-flight customer service, baggage claim, catering, frequent flier programs, and so on. Typically, these units are inwardly focused, built around their own internal legacy processes. By embracing customer-centric processes, transportation companies can use technology across the enterprise to improve the customer experience. Technology can help transportation companies present a single, unified image to their customers, from the time customers buy to the time they ride, sail or fly, and from the moment they decide to ship a package to the time their intended recipient receives that shipment. As Sir Rod Eddington of British Airways states: "You have to change your processes and be prepared to adopt smart systems. Otherwise, the efficiencies will elude you."

Dr. Frank Appel, CEO of DHL Logistics and Management and Board Member of Deutsche Post WorldNet, reinforces the importance of process innovation built around the customer. "Quality has two components," he notes, "a highly talented employee base on one hand and industrialized processes for all products on the other. Industrialization does not only mean to standardize all physical processes and operations, but also to strengthen one of the most important customer touch points—information."

Redefining institutional collaboration

The final piece of the capacity-optimization puzzle is the need for increased collaboration between the various public and private entities with a stake in the transportation industry. Dr. Richard John, Senior Technical Advisor at the John A. Volpe National Transportation Systems Center, writes: "The changing concepts for effective transportation decision-making include movement from exclusive to inclusive participation." He also notes that "one side cannot be seen as winning the war," and that shared gains across all stakeholders are essential for the future of the transportation industry.

The transportation industry faces tremendous challenges in the next several years, and how the industry responds to these challenges will have long-term implications for the global economy.

"One of the key challenges we face," writes Dr. David Pang, CEO of the Airport Authority of Hong Kong, "is that the flow is becoming ever more complex. This is further complicated by the fact that different parties in the chain have different priorities. These different elements must be pulled together to make them flow as if they were one single chain." Through greater collaboration among governments, regulatory bodies, private companies, infrastructure operators, and customers, the transportation industry can increase awareness of the critical issues, provide the impetus for process innovation and technology deployment, help establish open market regulations, and effectively increase capacity.

Contributors to this book agree that government plays a vital role in facilitating the evolution of transportation systems, particularly with respect to security and safety policies; but opinions are mixed about the extent and nature of that role. Many believe industry advances should be left to market forces, while others would like to see government play a more active role by setting standards and providing incentives that encourage innovation. Most agree that the optimal solution lies somewhere in the middle: public and private entities must collaborate.

Weighing in on the market forces side, Sir Rod Eddington of British Airways notes: "If governments get out of the way, it makes for a stronger aviation industry. The strongest airlines in Asia and the Middle East are new carriers in those countries who are free from government regulation. Mindless government regulation and interference in the economic realities of the industry are very counterproductive for both the transportation sector and airlines alike."

On the government-intervention side, the European Commission is moving forward with transportation policies and initiatives to drive the opening of airline routes to additional carriers and the integration of a unified rail infrastructure. David Neeleman of JetBlue notes: "Technology on its own cannot make the improvements the industry needs. The mismatches between the capabilities of the planes and the ground, plus the time lag involved in changing the ground-based infrastructure, are all growing, and the government needs to take the lead."

Jeffrey Shane of the U.S. Department of Transportation sums up the situation this way: "The vision of a high-technology infrastructure brimming with creativity and innovation, and delivering more productivity gains, will be realized only if transportation and business leaders are prepared to join in waging a sustained fight for change."

The future of transportation: next steps

The transportation industry faces tremendous challenges in the next several years, and how the industry responds to these challenges will have long-term implications for the global economy. No longer can we rely on slow, expensive infrastructure investments or demand-modulation strategies. Demand is growing too rapidly for these strategies to work. We must find better ways to use existing infrastructure.

Technologies critical to improving capacity—such as broadband connectivity and sensing equipment—are already becoming less expensive and easier to deploy. When technologies reach this stage of maturity, widespread implementation quickly follows. We expect this conventional wisdom to hold true in the transportation industry as well. The vast majority of companies will pilot these key technologies in the next two to five years, with full-scale rollout a few years later.

But for these technologies to bring about true breakthroughs in capacity optimization, two parallel efforts must also take place. First, key stakeholders must aggressively reengineer their own organizational processes to become more customer-centric, moving away from the legacy, inward-facing processes of the past quarter century.

Second, these stakeholders, both public and private, must collaborate with each other to increase awareness of the issues facing the industry, improve security within and among the different sectors of the industry, and establish various open-market regulations. Whether industry leaders will allow market forces to prevail or accept government intervention is uncertain. What is certain is that collaboration and agreement on strategy are required to achieve the goal of capacity optimization.

The essays in this book not only raise awareness of the critical issues facing the transportation industry in the next few years, but also stimulate debate and provide pragmatic advice on different approaches to meeting these challenges. We hope you find the essays inspiring and thought provoking. Above all, we hope they spur you to join the debate on the future of this vital industry.

The authors of this essay can be contacted at
praj@cisco.com, shoda@cisco.com, and hlock@cisco.com

Operators

Innovation through simplification

Sir Rod Eddington I CEO, British Airways, UK

Simplification and the use of technology have been fundamental to the process changes that have helped drive efficiency into British Airways. If you leave your processes the same, while aiming for greater efficiency by taking people out of the business, all you do is overload those who remain. Otherwise you have to change your processes and be prepared to adopt smart systems, otherwise the efficiencies will elude you.

Historically, businesses have acquired technology and altered it to suit their processes. Today's technology is different. At BA we have had to undertake a massive simplification drive, adjusting our processes to meet the systems rather than changing the systems to meet the processes.

One of the things that our CIO, Paul Coby, said a couple of years ago was: "We will make our processes so simple that customers can choose to do them for themselves."

So technology has changed how we communicate with our customers. People don't need to ring up the call centre to get their Frequent Flyer point balance or change their seat assignment. They can do it all online.

We have simplified our fare structure. In order to drive our fares online, we needed to reduce massively the number of fare types with their complex conditions. It would have been impossible or very costly to automate the previous structure.

That simplification then allows us to introduce innovations such as self-service kiosks. And we are supporting the introduction of a worldwide scheme for baggage-tracking using Radio Frequency Identification (RFID) technology. This means no more baggage labels to get removed, torn, or misread, which helps ensure that fewer passenger bags go missing, and results in greater efficiencies.

We have simplified the hardware too. The fewer the aircraft types you have, the simpler the business becomes. Every time you add a new aeroplane, you need new spares, inventory, simulators, and training processes. So we have cut the number of aircraft types we fly and now have five fewer aircraft types than we had in 2001.

Technology also changes the hardware itself. For example, we recently saw the first flight of the Airbus A380, and Boeing is starting production of the 787 soon. These aeroplanes are a world away from the machines that were flying when I joined the industry. Not only are they computer designed, they are computer manufactured as well. That changes the whole construction process; the technology inside the aeroplane, the way it communicates with the ground and with passengers on board.

1.1

However, we still fly people from point A to point B—in that sense nothing has changed. Yet 60 or 70 years ago, if you flew from Hong Kong to London, it took you a week in a flying boat. Every night the plane would land on a lake or river and you stayed in a hotel. The next day you set off again. Today, you can have dinner in Hong Kong, fly non-stop to London, and have breakfast there. So airframe, engine, and other technical innovations have changed the physical nature of what we can do.

> We have had to undertake a massive simplification drive, adjusting our processes to meet the systems rather than changing the systems to meet the processes.

And once you were in your seat, there used to be nothing to do. When in-flight movies were introduced, everyone watched the same movie on a screen on the bulkhead. You watched what the airline provided, when the airline provided it. Now you can choose which movie you watch, or you can watch sports, kids' programmes, or even check your emails in-flight.

Perhaps the biggest change has been the price. Fifty years ago only the rich and famous could afford to fly. Now everybody can fly around the world, so innovation has revolutionised the industry in many ways.

You need to be big enough to exploit good ideas wherever you find them, from inside or outside the business, and apply them, winnowing out the ones that take you backwards. At BA we have taken ideas from other airlines, from others in the transport business, from car hire and hotel companies, as well as from consumer products and manufacturing—from anywhere. You need to create an atmosphere where people are encouraged to bring their ideas to the table for discussion.

It takes time and is hard work. For instance, I have personally hosted events for our regular first-class customers to discuss the future of first class and what their needs are.

One of the best results of that philosophy was flat beds. We were the first airline to put flat beds in first class in the mid-1990s, and the first to put them in business class in 2000. That idea came from customers.

Change and innovation are endemic—quite simply, if you cannot adapt, you will not survive. Organisations such as Pan-American, TWA, Sabena and Swissair all failed because they were unable to adjust to a changing business environment.

It is all too easy, when the numbers start to improve and the external environment seems a little less hostile, to sit back just a little and relax. That is the moment when your competitors—the ones who continue to change—come from behind and run right over you. The lesson is never to declare victory, because the race is never finished.

So you need to be constantly looking at how to improve efficiency, to give your customers better value for their money and to create a better working environment for your people.

If you are to innovate, you need first to understand your customers. In any business, there is no substitute for that. Many airlines pay the idea lip service, but our strongest competitors—such as Cathay Pacific, Singapore Airlines, and Virgin Atlantic—are like us. They have also simplified, and also work hard at listening to and understanding their customers, so we need to work hard to stay ahead.

During my time at the company, BA and the industry faced their darkest moments. Despite that, we have emerged better, stronger, and fitter. There have been some painful decisions to be taken along the way, something all at BA can be proud of.

The challenge is how to retain that momentum because stopping to relax is fatal. Take Ford and General Motors. They confront huge problems at the moment. These two major industry icons are arguably in life-threatening territory right now. Coming up behind are companies such as Toyota, Nissan, Hyundai, and Kia. More efficient European producers have helped make that industry more competitive than ever, and soon the Chinese will start making cars. Yet there was a time when GM, Ford, and Chrysler dominated the global automotive business.

Further afield, China and India currently have little impact on global aviation as they are relatively small markets internationally. Clearly that will change hugely in the next decade. The Chinese and Indians are increasingly global players in other industries, which suggests that aviation will follow.

The old, established industrialised nations are having to realise that the challenges coming from places like India and China are real, not just in manufacturing but in services as well. There are enormous opportunities, too, so smart companies and countries will look to explore those possibilities. For BA of course, that trade growth means the likelihood of more traffic to and from China and India.

The aviation industry is deeply in the red. It has lost more money—US$35 billion—since 9/11 than ever before.

It is a bleak situation for a number of reasons. The most immediate is the attack on New York's World Trade Center—which resulted in a huge drop in airline travel—and its aftermath. The Gulf War and the resulting high price of fuel, together with SARS, have combined to paint a depressing background for any airline executive.

1.1

But there are more structural problems, too. The industry is heavily fragmented and overly regulated. Since the industry began, every country has felt that it needed its own national flag carrier. As a result, there are some 100 to 200 significant airlines around the world, depending on how you measure it. In no other established industry are there so many players. You will not find 100 to 200 car manufacturing companies or hotel chains. All those long-established industries have undergone substantial consolidation.

> ### Mindless government regulation and interference in the economic realities of the industry are very counter-productive for both the transportation sector and airlines alike.

Government is one of the biggest barriers to the economic development of the aviation industry. Governments get in the way. Mindless government regulation and interference in the economic realities of the industry are very counter-productive for both the transportation sector and airlines alike

After 9/11, the US Government threw billions of taxpayers' dollars at the airline industry. The result confirmed what we already knew: state subsidies do not work. They encourage the wrong sort of behaviours and are a waste of taxpayers' money.

Governments should stay out of the business of who owns an airline, about where it flies, about what it charges, about whether it serves sandwiches or not. The marketplace should decide those things, not governments.

Subsidies distort. Historically, rail has always been hugely subsidised. In the old days, train transport was used by everyone. This meant government had licence to subsidise it hugely and it continues to receive government support.

Aviation, on the other hand, was for the rich and famous, and so has never had that level of government support. Despite that, the ownership and control provisions in the bi-lateral agreements under which airlines fly, forces them to be nation-state owned and controlled. Unsubsidised airlines then find themselves competing against subsidised trains. That is an unhealthy dynamic. It creates an inequality and is my main criticism of government intervention.

If governments get out of the way, it makes for a stronger aviation industry. The strongest airlines in Asia and the Middle East are new carriers which are free from government intervention. It accounts for the success of organisations like Cathay Pacific and Singapore Airlines, which have taken advantage of the opportunities that a laissez-faire world presents.

It is absolutely right, however, that governments have a strong role to play in safety and security regulation, because they are critical issues where a level playing field is essential. Governments and airline executives need to work closely together in that area.

Technology allows us to continue product innovation at an unparalleled pace.

Government also has a legitimate role in transport integration. We need a sensible strategy for transport, no matter who owns it, which involves the integration of road, rail, and air. It means people can travel on mixed-mode, integrated transport systems, which I believe is fundamental to an efficient transportation sector now and into the future. And there is no doubt that, for shorter journeys, the train is a perfectly sensible alternative. Airports like Frankfurt and Charles de Gaulle in Paris have high-speed rail links to the airport, for example.

Governments also need to remove constraints. They should fix items such as insufficient or poor infrastructure. Other than that, I think governments should stay out of the way.

Real-world examples exist. In some countries, governments have accepted that challenge, such as Singapore and Hong Kong, where the governments have built new airports. They have created an environment where private enterprise can flourish and the economic benefits to the peoples of those places are clear. We can see that in many places in the US as well, where the government has recognised it has an enabling role that includes the provision of appropriate infrastructure.

Governments are also involved, quite naturally, in international environmental initiatives—so here they do have a role to play.

Increasingly, the environment is a major issue for the aviation industry, as it should be for every industry. All parts of the industry have worked hard over the last 30 years to deliver aeroplanes that make less noise and generate less pollution. It all goes a long way towards helping to keep aviation viable.

I believe very strongly, too, that airlines need to be involved in a sensible emissions trading scheme. Unless airlines are seen to meet their environmental responsibilities, it will be very difficult in the medium and longer terms to grow.

I would hope that, through the International Civil Aviation Organisation and the International Air Transport Association, the two global regulatory bodies, we could develop common regulations to ensure that all airlines play by the same rules, no matter where they are based.

1.1

Consolidation is essential. The industry needs to behave in a more rational and economic manner if it is to have a future. Who the winners and losers will be is hard to say. The important thing is that government needs to remove itself from the process and allow the market to decide.

More certain is the onward march of technology. Moore's Law said effectively that the power of technology would double about every two years. It has held true for a remarkable period of time. So technology allows us to continue product innovation at an unparalleled pace.

Assuming this pace will continue, it is difficult to envisage what will happen in 20 years' time. Go back 30 years and the rate at which new products were bought to market, at which technology changed and allowed early adopters to build a better mousetrap has transformed this and other industries. Even flat beds, TV and games, email, and phones on board would have been unimaginable in 1970. The good news is that there will be innovations—the passenger experience both in the air and on the ground will change markedly. We just cannot foresee them, as technology changes so quickly.

Parameters that look unlikely to change are that people will still be flying at 80 per cent of the speed of sound and that fares will continue falling. The Boeing 747 and 777 and the Airbus A380 and A340 are major aeroplanes that are in commercial service either now or soon will be. All can cover very long distances, nonstop, quite comfortably. They do it much more efficiently, with lower seat-mile cost, making fares much cheaper in real terms, allowing many more people to fly.

Forty years ago, a round-the-world fare probably cost you somewhere between US$1,500 and US$2,000, a price that would buy you three months in a good hotel at around US$30 to US$40 a night. Today that round trip still costs you somewhere between US$1,500 and US$2,000 but that amount will buy you only four or five nights in that good hotel. That is the difference in real terms.

I just hope the industry does not continue to lose money at the rate of US$5 billion to US$6 billion a year, or it has a very bleak future.

About British Airways

British Airways is the world's second largest international airline, flying to over 550 destinations and carrying about 36 million passengers around the world.

The airline's two main operating bases are London's two main airports, Heathrow (the world's busiest international airport) and Gatwick. It employs over 47,472 staff worldwide, and British Airways group fleet comprises 290 aircraft.

British Airways is owned entirely by private investors.

1.1

Technology meets low-cost challenges

David Neeleman I CEO, JetBlue Airways, U.S.

JetBlue Airways started with three key tenets, which led to it becoming one of the profitable and expanding airlines in the United States. These were: to become the most efficient airline with the lowest cost, to have the best product, and to be the best-capitalized airline for its size.

So far we are on plan. We already have 78 airplanes—there will be 91 by the end of 2005—and we plan to add some 35 more over each of the next five years or so. With its new fleet of aircraft, JetBlue is ahead of much of its competition in terms of technology.

Given recent events, we watch the price of oil carefully like any airline. However, our new planes are more fuel efficient than most, so much so that I am of two minds about whether I want to see oil prices rise or fall. If oil falls to US$35 a barrel, we save a huge amount of money—but so do our competitors. If it goes up to US$85, because our planes burn 780 gallons an hour and can carry 156 people, we need only a US$10 average fare increase for every US$20 hike in the price per barrel. Our competitors are not as efficient, so it will cost them more.

Our biggest challenges by far are the joint problems of growing demand and infrastructure lag, which act as a brake on increases in traffic by limiting the number of planes that can fly in a given airway.

The airplanes are there. They have positioning capabilities using GPS tracking and plenty of other new technologies, so they could easily move to a free flight control system. The trouble is they have to interface with an antiquated air traffic system that we need to drag into the 21st Century if we are to increase throughput. If we cannot manage that, the Federal Aviation Administration (FAA) has predicted that we will see worsening congestion.

The other major brake on progress is a lack of runways. At heavily trafficked airports, planes are landing at 40-second intervals and there is no way to increase capacity without laying more asphalt on which to land the planes—and that is a very political problem. Traffic levels took a dip after 9/11 but they are now higher than in 2001, and rising. Yet it currently takes up to 20 years to build a new runway, if you include delays created by legal and political processes. Many sections of the population seem to want to stop new runways being built—environmentalists or people who live nearby—but they all want to fly places and they all want low fares. Today's planes are very quiet so noise is not a big problem; you have to live very close to an airport to hear it.

Fort Lauderdale is a good example of the problem. With south Florida the U.S.'s fastest-growing area, the New York-Fort Lauderdale route is the busiest in the U.S. The Florida airport has three runways, two of them paid for with taxpayers' money under the Air Improvement Program. Following pressure from local groups, the "not-in-my-backyard" people, represented by many of the local county commissions, initially decided the FAA should use only one of those runways. As usual, noise was said to be the problem. If the FAA decides to use the runways anyway, the local people threaten to sue—although there has been no test case yet. Gridlock results. Although the two closed runways have finally been given the green light to re-open, the real benefits will come on completion of an agreed plan to extend one of the runways, but that could take up to 10 years to complete.

1.2

> The only way to carry more people using existing infrastructure is to build bigger planes—and make better use of technology.

There are plenty of other examples, especially in Southern California. Airports at Orange County and Long Beach are slot-controlled, while the local council has voted not to expand Burbank Airport for a minimum of 10 years. Los Angeles International Airport is putting a brake on expansion just as another airport, an ex-military base in El Toro, is being sold off for development—it was a perfect position for an airport. The only facility that is not either full or that will admit any more flights is Ontario, and that is a distance from downtown Los Angeles.

A further challenge for us is growth in the number of smaller, commercial planes. Many 50-seat planes have been great for some communities but they are reaching saturation point. The problem is two-fold. They take more airspace because they fly slower and they cannot take off directly after a big airplane because of its turbulence wake. This means they use 1.5 times more airspace than a plane that holds three times as many people. At La Guardia and Washington Reagan National Airport, for example, a large percentage of big-jet slots are being used by small planes.

While building more infrastructure is not a practical solution today, the most obvious way of managing too much traffic is to raise fares and reduce the numbers of people traveling, but that is not a good policy for the U.S. We have to be practical and, with neither more runways nor a benevolent, Congress-mandated dictator who can just make things happen, the only way to carry more people using existing infrastructure is to build bigger planes— and make better use of technology.

More technology, more capacity

The big win from the use of technology will be free flight. Today, we string our aircraft in a line going from east to west. If one fixed point closes because of a thunderstorm, it shuts down the whole system. The best we can do today is use traffic alert/collision avoidance systems that work well with respect to planes nearby. The system knows exactly where each plane is and can even give instructions on what to do to avoid a collision.

Technology on its own cannot make the improvements the industry needs. The mismatch between the capabilities of the planes and the ground, plus the time lag involved in changing the ground-based infrastructure, are all growing, and government needs to take the lead.

With free flight, they would have hundreds of other routes from which to choose. This could work using technology with sophisticated algorithms to keep planes separated, instead of simply keeping planes several miles apart. Air traffic control should be able to insist that every plane is fitted with the device—even the weekend warriors. Every airplane in flight would broadcast its location using a special frequency. If a plane were to ask for clearance, everyone would be able to see everybody else. For general aviation, there would even be benefits in making the device free, so tiny planes could broadcast their position. The system could then predict potential conflicts 30 minutes ahead and adjust both airplanes' paths to ensure they keep a safe distance apart.

The FAA's Joint Planning and Development Office (JPDO) already believes that nothing less than the complete transformation of the U.S. air system is needed, and it could easily be accomplished. But there are so many vested interests, and so many people who use the system who refuse to pay for it.

JetBlue is a low-fare airline, so we are heavy users of technology to keep costs down, and that means maximizing asset utilization, both people and equipment.

We use technology from the minute the customer reserves a seat to the time they pull their bag off the carousel. About 80 per cent of our bookings are made over our own Website. Often, passengers want to make a change, so we have airport check-in kiosks that 40 per cent of passengers now use. The people who take reservations over the phone work from home rather than a call center. This helps the environment by reducing travel and traffic, and provides greater job satisfaction, which makes them happier people—technology makes that easy. Pilots no longer need to carry bulky manuals, as a laptop contains all the manuals. They can also use it for the calculations they need to make.

Technology assists on the operational side, too. We have in-house software that crunches all the eventualities and algorithms on how we should route aircraft, which planes to cancel, which to keep going—and how we put Humpty Dumpty back together again when a snowstorm wipes us out.

When on board, technology allows people to watch live television, and we will soon be adding 100 channels of XM satellite radio. Using the XM radio antenna, we can pipe current weather information into the cockpits, so pilots get more up-to-date weather than they can on their radar systems alone.

1.2

When it comes to security, technology gives us surveillance cameras in the cabin that the flight deck can monitor, so pilots just focus on flying the plane. On a broader level, clearly a plane is a more controlled environment than a subway or shopping mall, so I am fairly confident that we have that element under control.

Globally, though, I think the pendulum has probably swung a bit too far towards caution. Given 9/11, this is understandable. But today, with hardened cockpit doors, heightened passenger awareness, and surveillance cameras, I am not concerned anymore about someone commandeering an airplane with their bare hands or a sharp object. We also send every bag that enters the plane through explosive-detection devices so, again, I feel we have that under control.

For the future, I would like to see technology solve the problem of increasing flow through the passenger and luggage security systems—there is a great deal of technology in the works that could make things run a lot smoother.

Government needs to lead

Technology on its own cannot make the improvements the industry needs. The mismatch between the capabilities of the planes and the ground, plus the time lag involved in changing the ground-based infrastructure, are all growing, and government needs to take the lead.

It can enable the system to work more efficiently and even ensure that modernization is paid for. For example, leaving general aviation aside, the smaller commercial planes take up a disproportionate amount of airspace in relation to the number of people they move. In the U.S., anyone who files a flight plan has a right to be in the sky, but I believe they should pay for use of the system. Today, the only payment mechanism for planes in a controlled airspace area is fuel tax, which covers only some 2 to 3 percent of the budget for operating the system. Yet, depending on who you believe, they use between 20 and 30 per cent of the infrastructure.

Assuming they increased their contribution tenfold, it could pay for a complete overhaul of the system. You would need to convince the Treasury Department to raise US$20 billion to US$30 billion on the back of that revenue stream and, under tight scrutiny, dedicate the money specifically to modernizing the system with whatever technology the users and the Joint Planning and Development Office (JPDO) determine is best and most efficient.

Aviation is essentially a very simple operation—sometimes it gets more complicated than it needs to be. All we are doing is moving people from A to B and handing them back their bag.

Like most of us in the industry, I believe that, fundamentally, aviation will change little in the foreseeable future. The speed we travel is the same as it was when the first 707 took off and is likely to stay that way—you can go faster but you burn a lot more gas.

If you look at the past, improvements have been incremental, such as high by-pass engines that use a lot less fuel and are quieter. Boeing is working on the 787, which will use more composite materials—it will weigh less and be more economical. Little is likely to change drastically on the engine side either. Unfortunately, there are no alternative fuel sources, which our industry could badly use, so we need to continue squeezing more productivity from our jet fuel.

Changes resulting from technology will be exterior to us, primarily in air traffic control systems, in the construction of runways, and the ability to improve traffic flows; there is a lot of potential out there.

From the passenger's point of view, flying has barely changed in 45 years. The seats may have moved a little closer to your nose, but you have a tray table just as you had in 1960. What we have tried to do is make that experience different by offering more entertainment and connectivity to the outside world, and that will continue. However, I do not think passengers want people making phone calls on airplanes; like trains, nobody wants to have some guy chomping away on the phone when they're trying to read or sleep, and it is no different on a plane.

While the onboard experience is unlikely to change fundamentally, passengers will be able to book and check in online, go to the airport, and drop their bags off, as opposed to standing in line. Hopefully the flights will be more on time as traffic systems improve. And by then, we may have figured out a better way to pull bags off planes so that, when you get to the carousel, they are waiting for you. But first we need to find a better way of connecting the belly of the airplane with the carousel.

In terms of the company itself, we have 156-seat aircraft and we are buying 100-seaters, which provide better economics, allow us to fly into more new places, and fill the gap between 50- and 150-seat planes.

Aviation is essentially a very simple operation—sometimes it gets more complicated than it needs to be. All we are doing is moving people from A to B and handing them back their bag. That is the essence, so it is tough to innovate, to make it very different than that. But what has really surprised me is our customers' loyalty, so we must be doing something right: I pledge to keep trying to please each and every customer.

1.2

About JetBlue

JetBlue Airways is a low-fare, low-cost passenger airline, with a focus on providing high-quality customer service. It was founded in July 1999 by David Neeleman who, with three successful aviation businesses under his belt and having secured US$130 million in capital funding, decided the time was right to bring his airline formula to the world's largest aviation market—New York City. He announced his plan to launch a new airline that would bring "humanity back to air travel" and on February 11, 2000 JetBlue took to the air with the inauguration of service between New York City's John F. Kennedy International Airport and Fort Lauderdale. The airline now serves 32 cities in the United States and the Caribbean.

Technology and logistics: a natural partnership

Dr. Frank Appel I CEO, DHL Logistics and Management Board Member, Deutsche Post AG, Germany

From a global perspective, the logistics industry is still relatively immature, and shows unbalanced development across the different geographical regions. However, consolidation is a key trend and we see consistently growing market shares of top players. From this perspective, the market will consist of two types of players in the future: global players with extensive scale on the one hand and local/regional heroes with specialised, niche market capabilities on the other.

The key challenge for a global logistics player is to differentiate in the market, instead of just competing on the cheapest price. Despite the immaturity of the industry, customers in general are becoming more and more demanding and business processes remain complex. Besides the traditional shipping of goods from A to B, more and more customers request end-to-end visibility, optimised inventory, flexible distribution networks, transaction-based pricing, and so on. As a consequence of globalisation, customers look for logistics partners capable of providing this consistent service level across all regions.

> Customers in general are becoming more and more demanding and business processes remain complex.

The answer to the differentiation challenge therefore has to be quality. But what does quality mean for a global logistics provider? From my perspective, quality has two components: a highly talented employee base on the one hand and industrialised processes for all products on the other. In the end, companies that succeed in upgrading their intellectual capital while retaining their entrepreneurial spirit will be those that survive the coming shake-out.

We believe that two different types of people are required to run a logistics business.

When it comes to the day-to-day element of the business, you need entrepreneurs who can drive quality into the organisation. Any logistics organisation is only as good as the last consignment it delivers on time: be late or over-budget, and your reputation suffers. So our service relies entirely on day-to-day execution, and we depend on this type of person for our survival.

The other piece of the puzzle consists of more strategic thinkers. Running an operational department calls for different skills from those needed for designing a supply chain. R&D department people often see their job as innovation—the ability to revise and optimise the supply chain continually, rather than talking to customers or sales and marketing people.

The success lies in bringing these different pieces of the puzzle together. It is important that both cultures understand each other so that nobody feels threatened by the skills of the other—it should be like a good marriage. Success depends on being able to deploy both types of skills and engineer mutual respect on both sides.

1.3

Industrialisation not only means to standardise all physical processes and operations, but also to strengthen one of the most important customer touch points—information.

Information for a global business

Increasingly, globalisation of our customers leads to an increasing importance of global business information. Customers prefer to be proactively informed rather than to be confronted with surprises, as any kind of uncertainty has a price tag on it. Logistics players need to respond accordingly as this area has often been perceived as a somewhat grey area in the entire supply chain, full of unforeseen risks. We thus see it as a key differentiator to sell more information to the customer than others do. Mere transportation of items from A to B is just not enough—the service has to include the information that accompanies the shipment, too.

Customers tell us that, of course, they recognise that no logistics organisation can promise 100 per cent delivery—it simply is not humanly possible. There will always be unavoidable occurrences: the equipment breaks down, a traffic jam causes delays or an aeroplane needs emergency maintenance. Where fast information is important, however, customers have to know about those shipments that are not being delivered on time, as they themselves will need to pass the information quickly to their own customers.

As our customers globalise, we have industrialised our processes accordingly. In theory, at least, this leads to common standards around the globe. In practice, however, three hurdles make standardisation difficult.

Firstly, managing the constant change associated with globalisation is a tremendous challenge. Nobody anticipated this fast growth in globalisation that we are currently experiencing—its pace has really surprised us all. Companies are moving their plants ever faster round the planet—they are currently heading for China as one top-priority location—and logistics companies follow. But in view of long-term warehouse contracts, for instance, we need a structured and strategic approach in order to handle these moves.

Technology innovation is critical in terms of helping us manage and maintain an efficient infrastructure.

Cultural difference is another hurdle. One key characteristic that has to be observed is that logistics do not involve hardware, like a BlackBerry, easy to copy and make work in a different place in just the same way. The logistics industry is about people, with different cultures and local needs in differing local regulation environments. All these differences affect your ability to run the process, and to do it cost-effectively.

This means that if we move a manager from one place to another, we cannot be sure that he will be able to run the warehouse or gateway in the same way as before. Without plug and play, life is complex both for us and our customers. So one key challenge is to be adaptive to fast changes, and to develop globally standardised processes, with managers able to drive such a challenge.

The third issue applies to the IT infrastructure backbone that needs to be equally advanced and flexible to help keep control of a global business via accurate and real-time information. Our systems have to be adaptable, as not all our people speak English, and our handheld devices might, for example, be in Mandarin for China or Hindi for India. This backbone infrastructure, therefore, needs to allow us to move information easily from country to country. Strategically this means a change from legacy to global applications, with cheap and standardised infrastructure. We are talking here about one of the decisive future challenges common to many companies in all kinds of industries. Quality leadership and common standards will more and more depend on excellence and reliability in integrated networks.

Trading information

In maybe five to 10 years, we will not only be seen as a transportation company but also as an information trading company—which is what forwarding has become. Maximising the amount and quality of that information, and using it well, is more of an art than science.

Essentially, this process involves buying space on vessels and selling it to customers. With 100 per cent visibility of spot market prices on the system, the dispatcher, who decides how to ship a certain consignment, can use that information to help make the right decision.

With a light asset load, profitability in logistics depends on good deal-making. If a stockbroker takes early profits, he lowers the risk of losing if they fall, and it is more profitable in the long run. In our business, if you make commitments too far into the future or make the wrong commitments, you can lose a lot of money. Thus, follow the market, be flexible, combine the best information with the best judgement and, in the long run, profits will result.

This requires fast, real-time information. For instance, in buying cargo space, if we know the profit levels on a second-by-second basis, the dispatcher or import/export office can make immediate decisions on pricing. The system will just give the dispatcher a range of options to offer to customers while he is on the phone to them.

In contract logistics, inventory management is key. We use information management, planning and monitoring—that means different kinds of information that allow supply chain optimisation. And here economies of scale can be achieved by using IT forecasting systems across multiple customers.

1.3

The remaining physical transport piece of the equation—transporting goods from A to B, is then a commodity decision and consists mainly of managing subcontractors.

Harnessing technology

Since our business is as much about trading information as about shipping products, IT needs to be tightly managed to make sure we are concentrating our efforts and investments in the right areas.

Key to that is forming a global IT team that is able to deliver. Becoming a real leader in the transportation and IT industries heavily depends on developing the right structures, and we have already taken steps in that direction.

Technology innovation is critical in terms of helping us manage and maintain an efficient infrastructure. So we are always asking questions, ranging from what we should outsource, to which technology services we could be providing for our customers in the future. We also use vendors' resources to help develop and maintain applications and, sooner or later, we will outsource that infrastructure.

But the more IT becomes mission-critical, the more important it is that we keep a certain level of knowledge in-house. That means we retain a kernel of intellectual capacity for systems design. This then leads us to other value-added businesses. We have a presence and provide commodity IT services in more than 220 countries and territories. Bundle these IT services with logistics transportation services and we are perfectly positioned. It is part of our vision to become the intelligence that glues those pieces together.

While technology is tremendously important, our organisation remains very much a people business, with intense local interaction. The better the information we generate, the easier it is for people on the ground to make the right decisions. The greater price transparency we have, the better we can manage our systems and help customers get better value for their money.

It has become a mantra that the most important thing for business is to develop common standards for information and communications, especially vertically, up and down the supply chain. I doubt that this issue will ever be fully resolved.

The problem with standards is that they can hinder innovation. Once a standard is agreed, vendors start developing the next one, in the drive to be first out of the gate.

In the future, I believe that software technology will probably be developed in a way that is more or less self-organising, and will translate information easily. Today's databases are stupid; the IT world needs to find a way to ensure that the same information is presented in different ways, depending on usage or need.

However, the IT industry is a very immature world. Mass IT is only around 30 years old. When IT reaches the maturity of today's car industry, I cannot imagine what that means. I am sure that it will have undergone tremendous change.

1. TEU = Twenty-foot
Equivelent Units.

Translated to the logistics industry, there is room for innovation in shipping, too. In the future, speed will become more and more critical. Instead of 8,000-TEU[1] ships—the size of the latest ones now—we may perhaps use 500-TEU ships. Three times faster, they could open up a new market segment—slower than air freight, faster than traditional shipping, as well as cheaper and more flexible. They could go anywhere, to small harbours as well as large ones, and even inland by river.

Logistics is definitely an industry with incredible future potential and lots of new dimensions. Today's logistics needs comprise more than just the initial need of transportation from A to B and mean a huge operational and cultural challenge. Global customers need integrated global logistics partners with local knowledge, customised relationship management, a broad service portfolio along the entire supply chain and improved visibility through customer-friendly IT interfaces.

We see Deutsche Post World Net as well positioned for this challenge.

About DPWN and DHL

As the world's leading logistics group, Deutsche Post World Net (DPWN) integrates Deutsche Post, DHL and Postbank companies to offer tailored, customer-focused solutions for the management and transport of goods, information and payments through a global network combined with local expertise. DPWN aims to be a one-stop provider, offering the full range of logistics services—from document transport to complete supply chain management—to its customers worldwide. Some 380,000 employees in more than 220 countries and territories worldwide generated revenues of EUR 43 billion ($58 billion) in 2004.

The DHL brand integrates its Express and Logistics activities. The Logistics business focuses on Freight Forwarding and Contract Logistics.

1.3

How customers are reshaping our industry

John Mullen | Joint CEO, DHL Express and Management Board Member, Deutsche Post AG, Germany

The express delivery business has undergone seismic changes in the last 20 years, most of it driven by changes in patterns of customer behaviour and demand, such as outsourcing the supply chain, as well as a perceived need to exactly match the customer's needs as much as possible.

Supply chain outsourcing does not just involve shipping goods. For one customer, for example, DHL provides a complete credit card replacement service—from the first distress phone call, to cutting the new card, to delivery of the new card to the user. We are also working on sophisticated products such as trade finance and inventory financing solutions as well as no-fault testing and repair and return, particularly for the IT industry. Such services have a lot of future and add considerable value for both the customer and ourselves.

The big enabler has been technology innovation. It has, for instance, allowed customers to increase the integration of their systems with ours. In the US, over 80 per cent of our customers' systems transact electronically with DHL, although in Asia the figure is still closer to 30 or 40 per cent. However, this volume is growing and that means our services are moving beyond just track and trace. Instead, we are seeing an integration of customers' and suppliers' data flows, allowing customers to understand the impact that a particular product has on their stock levels, distribution, warehousing and re-ordering processes. All these things require deep data integration.

But by outsourcing those processes, customers are taking greater operational risks. Dismantling warehouses means they are abandoning management of their supply chain and placing their trust in others. It is a very hard decision to reverse—and makes our role all the more critical to the customer's success.

The time footprint has changed dramatically, too. In international shipping, a three-to-four-day delivery was the best that could be expected only a decade or so ago. By using dedicated freight aircraft, the industry brought that down to one or two days for short-haul deliveries, which was pretty revolutionary at the time. Now we can handle overnight deliveries anywhere within the range of a modern aeroplane. That is a good example of how the dynamics of the industry have changed. It used to be the case that shippers would present their network to the customer, who would have to take it or leave it. If they fitted the mould, great; if they didn't, tough. Today there is increasing pressure from customers for us to change our network to mirror their

requirements from a distribution point of view. They ask: "This is our specific requirement, can you supply it?"

Customers are also driving convergence between integrators and forwarders. The integrator model is the fixed network, while forwarders can pick and choose from a menu of all the world's airlines and operations to tailor a customer-specific service.

> DHL operates in a global environment and today change is being driven both by major economic growth in countries such as China... and by technology innovation.

1.4

Forwarding can represent savings to the customer of 300 to 400 per cent, so as a generalisation, urgent samples and critical parts go by express, and finished goods by forwarding. As a result, forwarders and integrators are responding to customer pressure for express features at forwarding prices, and vice versa.

The growth of consumer-based, online commerce is also affecting distribution networks. Today, products delivered to consumers tend to be relatively small objects, such as CDs, but with the expansion of online retailing, the variety of goods is expanding. This will have knock-on effects, such as air pollution and congestion caused by truck movements in residential areas. Local authorities are keen to control such movements by, for example, restricting vehicular access, making it more problematic to get a truck down residential streets. Consequently, the trend is to make deliveries using smaller vehicles from a greater number of smaller hubs.

Taking a global outlook

DHL operates in a global environment. Today, change is being driven both by major economic growth in countries such as China, especially compared to more traditional markets like Europe and the Americas, and by technology innovation. Both trends have major ramifications for our business.

Parcel traffic constitutes 85 per cent of our express revenues as people send fewer documents than before—they use fax or email instead. Fortunately for us, the result of the shift from lightweight documents to heavyweight parcels and general distribution is that revenues increase, even if shipment volume growth slows.

Global growth in the cargo market is running at around 6 to 8 per cent. Typically, the overnight air express market has tended to grow around 50 per cent faster. However, that hides large regional differences.

In the US, the overnight air express market has seen slow growth for the last few years, but this is particularly affected by the worldwide slowing of document volumes, whereas the core parcel market in the US is still growing.

> As our industry becomes increasingly commoditised, we would rather add value than cut prices, so technology will be at the heart of the innovations that enable us to make those differentiations.

In Asia, the document market is still showing growth of around 2 to 3 per cent, driven by the 10- to 12-per cent plus growth in developing markets like China. The established economies of Hong Kong, Singapore and Australia show zero or negative document growth, but parcel growth across the board is 20 per cent plus, and that trend looks set to continue.

Europe would still appear to have double-digit parcel growth. The market is still growing and is probably one step down in sophistication from the United States, which is the clear forerunner of most trends and development.

Managing growth in the East

The express business in Asia is in the enviable situation of increasingly demonstrating all the traits of modern sophisticated economies, while still growing like a developing market in almost all locations.

China is driving regional growth. It is becoming a global economic force, and its rate of growth is without precedent for an economy of this size. We are hiring over 1,000 new staff and opening 10 to 15 new depots every year just to handle this extraordinary growth. China is fast becoming a major consumer market in its own right, whilst its burgeoning export capabilities are sucking in imports of components and materials needed for its factories, especially from Asia. These are then exported to Europe and the US as finished goods. For a transport and distribution company like DHL, of course, this is a huge opportunity as we are well-positioned to take advantage of these trade flows wherever they occur.

A big influence in future will be the development of North Asia—Japan, China, Korea, Hong Kong and Taiwan—as a trading block in its own right. This area is forecast to constitute about 20 per cent of the world's GDP by around 2015.

This will affect both distribution patterns and the development of our industry. Currently, most of us in this industry deploy hub and spoke operations. For example, DHL has a hub in Hong Kong and, if an item is to go from Tokyo to Shanghai, it goes from Tokyo to Hong Kong, then back up to Shanghai. The huge growth in the northern triangle means the region will need its own hubs and direct flights in the very near future.

Future innovations

As our industry becomes increasingly commoditised, we would rather add value than cut prices, so technology will be at the heart of the innovations that enable us to make those differentiations.

For instance, we plan to increase automation of existing manual practices, interacting electronically with all our customers on all transactions. Similarly, five to 10 years from now, almost all of the driver's day will be planned electronically, reshaping driver routes and process flows in realtime to suit the changing trends of customers' traffic.

Radio Frequency Identification (RFID) is a technology of the future and will change our industry substantially by adding huge efficiencies. Although the cost of global deployment will be significant, efficient implementation will certainly deliver competitive advantage. The most significant current challenge is the adoption of agreed global standards. A global, mandated standard would save significant time and money for all concerned, and while the industry is trying to collaborate, a wide range of players will be touched by RFID, from suppliers to customers, which makes it a tougher and longer process.

1.4

As a result, I believe that it is likely that we will get there by using multistandard equipment that can read RFIDs across vendor and country boundaries, in the same way that tri-band mobile phones work across different frequencies.

About DPWN and DHL

As the world's leading logistics group, Deutsche Post World Net (DPWN) integrates Deutsche Post, DHL and Postbank companies to offer tailored, customer-focused solutions for the management and transport of goods, information and payments through a global network combined with local expertise. DPWN aims to be a one-stop provider, offering the full range of logistics services—from document transport to complete supply chain management—to its customers worldwide. Some 380,000 employees in more than 220 countries and territories worldwide generated revenues of EUR 43 billion ($58 billion) in 2004.

The DHL brand integrates its Express and Logistics activities. The Logistics business focuses on Freight Forwarding and Contract Logistics.

Infrastructure

Going with the flow

Dr. David J. Pang | CEO, Airport Authority Hong Kong

There is a tendency to think about airports primarily in terms of the function they serve. You can look at Hong Kong International Airport, for example, and focus on the fact that it expects to serve 40 million passengers and handle some 3.4 million tons of cargo this year. But an airport is much more than that: it is really the centre of multiple flows. Ferries bring passengers in by sea; trains, buses and cars carry them by land and aeroplanes move them by air. When people flow, they create economic activities that benefit various parties, and when products are moved from a place where they are in abundance to a place where there is a shortage, their value is maximised. In short, when people flow and goods flow, it creates wealth.

Transportation has been enhancing this flow for centuries. In the 18th Century, ports made the most significant contribution to these flows. In the 19th Century, it was rail, and in the last century it was road. I believe that in the 21st Century, the aviation industry will be the predominant enabler.

As an airport operator, our role is to continue to enhance the flow of people, goods and information, and to make the flow as efficient, reliable and safe as possible. To do so, we need to deploy a combination of technologies and services, and we have to overcome a number of practical obstacles. We consider ourselves to be one of the engines of economic growth, so our ability to carry out this role will be critical to the future prosperity of the community.

Integrating the chain

One of the key challenges we face is that the flow is becoming ever more complex. Growing volumes of people and cargo are passing through; more and more places are being connected to the airport through multimodal transport, or through our airport as the hub, and there are more players involved. So the way this chain is integrated is a critical success factor. These different elements must be pulled together to make them flow as if they were one single chain.

Consider the way we ship cargo. The chain starts with a business that wants to ship a product. The goods are collected and transported by truck to a forwarder, which then takes them to the cargo terminal. The airline flies the product to the appropriate airport, where it is loaded onto a truck and taken to the final destination. As an airport, we play a central role as one link in that chain. But to make the chain as efficient and reliable as possible, we need to have visibility from the beginning to the end—someone needs to be

integrating the whole flow and making sure that all the players in the chain are doing their part to make it effective. I believe that the airport is well placed to be the integrator.

If we look at the passenger's point of view, when you leave your hotel room in Hong Kong, we want to make sure your trip from the hotel to the airport is pleasant. If you wait a long time for transport or there is a lot of traffic on the road and you almost miss your flight, your perception of the entire chain will be affected. Likewise, when you get to the airport, the airline check-in service needs to be pleasant and efficient; the restaurant you use should provide good, quality food; we need to ensure that we have the right mix of shops to match your tastes; your baggage has to be put on the right aircraft and the flight itself has to be on time. When you are on the plane, we want you to have a pleasant experience—polite flight attendants, quality entertainment, a pleasant environment and good food. And if you fly into our airport, we cannot afford for our immigration people to be unpleasant or slow, or our customs people to be ineffective.

2.1

> As an airport operator, our role is to continue to enhance the flow of people, goods and information, and to make the flow as efficient, reliable and safe as possible.

Many people play a role in this chain to form all of these experiences, but airports' biggest role is that of integrator. After all, we have a vested interest in this; if you have a bad experience on your way to the airport, it will taint your perspective of the airport itself.

This is further complicated by the fact that different parties in the chain have different priorities. The airlines and the airport, for example, are partners and cannot function without one another, but their fundamental drivers are different. Private airlines ultimately have to satisfy their shareholders. Airports, whether publicly or privately owned, have to satisfy a wider range of stakeholders. We are publicly owned, so we have to satisfy Hong Kong taxpayers. But we also have to ensure that the local community is happy, and we need to satisfy the 243 companies operating at the airport, which include the airlines, the retail stores and all of the other associated businesses. And above all, we have to satisfy passengers and cargo customers.

The challenges of implementing technology

Information is critically important in any form of transportation, and particularly in aiding this flow. The more complex the flow becomes, the more important information and communications become. Technology is crucial—it helps us to enhance the flow and to make it efficient, more reliable and safer.

One of the challenges of implementing technology is that reliability is critically important for an airport—nobody wants to be a guinea pig for new products or services. Rather than jumping at the newest model, airports prefer to see how it works and be sure that it is robust enough for their environment. As a result, we do not always adopt technology as fast as other environments.

It is not the technology itself that is the problem— it is a question of finding the money to install it everywhere it needs to be.

The second issue is that information technologies and communications techniques need to be standardised to be effective. Fifty years ago we did not even talk to people in other countries. Today, whether you live in an isolated rural community or in the middle of a bustling city, you can find out what's going on around the world through the Internet. But all of our communications need to be compatible; an aeroplane needs to communicate in the same way when it arrives at its destination airport as it did when it departed. And the information that we send from one place to another has to be in a language that both can understand.

This means that when a new technology emerges, it presents a major challenge for us because we need every airport in the world to use it. But airports are very capital-intensive businesses—the runways, the terminal buildings, everything you touch is very expensive. Every city and country has to put money into the airport, and regardless of how rich they are, resources are always limited, particularly given that the airport has to compete with other sectors for investment. As a result, some areas may be able to implement technology faster than others, but the areas where resources are constrained inevitably slow down global uptake. It is not the technology itself that is the problem—it is a question of finding the money to install it everywhere it needs to be.

Today, 195 airports around the world have been privatised, including six in China, and this presents new opportunities to seek out funds. Generally speaking, if you can demonstrate that you have a true growth opportunity, it should be possible to secure financial backing from the private sector so long as you have a credible plan for generating profit. This is a growing trend, and it is an issue that all publicly funded airports will ultimately need to address.

Despite these constraints, we have come a long way in a short time. Twenty years ago, you could not check in a bag direct to New York from China; today, that is a straightforward process. Likewise, you can travel through Paris, Calcutta, New York and Hong Kong without even speaking any of the local languages. Processes are very similar at every airport, from the questions they ask at the check-in counter onwards. And just as important, we are speeding up the rate of improvement through technology; what took 10 years to happen previously may well take only two years in the future.

Key emerging technologies

Fifteen or 20 years from now we will inevitably have more traffic—or more flow—through our airport. This will be fuelled partly by population growth in Asia. People tend to think of high-growth countries such as China and India as manufacturers and exporters, but it is important to bear in mind that they consume goods as well, and this mix is the core of all economic activities. To achieve it, people and goods have to move.

2.1

We will be relying on new technologies to help manage this growth. All of our processes and procedures will have to be more efficient, and we will need to think about all the different areas where we can make improvements. We may need new check-in procedures, for example—perhaps passengers will be able to do it from home rather than from a specific physical area at the airport. Gradually, I think the airport will evolve into an e-airport as the level of IT adoption grows.

A number of technologies are going to play an important role in this equation going forward. Radio Frequency Identification (RFID), for example, will be a key component; wherever there is a flow, you need to be able to identify and track the various elements in it, and provide sufficient transparency so that you can monitor and continually improve it. RFID serves that purpose, particularly on the cargo and baggage side, helping us manage and move information relating to individual items. The problem, as with all technologies, is that it has to be globally compatible. We have already started testing RFID and using it at Hong Kong International Airport in a limited way, but universal adoption will take a little time. Gradually, as the usage level increases across all industries, the costs will go down and that will help drive the spread of the technology.

We are also starting to test biometrics, which potentially will be a powerful tool to help make the whole aviation system more secure. Biometrics can be used in multiple ways, from check-in to immigration and even boarding. Some airports in Europe are already using it, although we are not quite ready to do so ourselves. The challenge for biometrics, of course, is reliability. Because we are using it for security, people need to be convinced that all possible risks have been eliminated and that it is totally secure; if your credit card number is stolen, you get a new card. You cannot do that with fingerprints or irises.

A third technology that is becoming ever more important is inter-networking. When we talk about managing the flow, we are really talking about integrating a large number of diverse components, many of them very complicated. For example, if we look at the way we exchange information with our customers, our systems today are not fully integrated, which means passengers have to find information from the airport and then look for separate information sources supplied by the airlines. What they really want is one single information feed that is reliable, and presented in a way that meets their needs.

SARS will not be the last crisis we will face; it may be a different virus, so together we learn how to deal with it in a better way, by using technology.

When you have 243 different partners in the same environment, many of them with different goals and answering to the interests of different stakeholders, effective communications become essential. It is not actually that difficult to achieve a common goal; the key is to make sure that, rather than looking at all the differences among us, we look instead at what we have in common. We all want more people to come through our airport, and we all want more cargo to come through—so our collective aim must be to enhance the overall experience for those customers. As the integrator in the chain, our role is to pull all of these different information pieces together, and inter-networking technology is an important tool in helping us do so.

Finally, I believe that technology has an important role to play in helping us deal with crises. The experiences of 9/11 in the United States and SARS in Asia have taught us important lessons. People always have a fear of the unknown, and these two incidents really helped us understand that where there is fear, it very quickly drives people into self-segregation—which means you either slow down or even stop the flow. That is the worst thing that can happen to a business like ours. Crises come and go, of course, and we truly believe that the flow of people and goods will continue regardless, but we do not want to face disruption on this scale.

SARS was not the last crisis we will face; next time, it may be a different virus, so together we need to learn how to deal with it in a better way, by using technology. I believe our mission is to build up our capability to better enhance the flow and to ensure that it is not interrupted. When there is no flow, there is no economic activity, no growth and no wealth being created—a major challenge for all of us.

The people factor

Technology itself has almost unlimited potential—the bottleneck is really the people. People and technology have to advance together, and we need everyone to participate in the benefits, not just part of the population. You cannot be satisfied if half of the world's population uses the Internet today but the other half has no access; at some point, we will have to go back to hook up those people and bring them along with us, because we live in one highly interconnected world.

People today cannot imagine living without electricity or without computers, and we have become very reliant on them; last year, the whole air transportation system stopped for two hours at Heathrow Airport because a computer broke down. But while no one disputes the convenience factor and how much we rely on technology, it is important to ask whether it is making us happier. I am sure convenience brings some degree of happiness—but if I give you more and more convenience, will that actually make you happier and happier?

2.1

This is one of the limitations of technology—there is a difference between how fast we are able to go and how fast we actually want to go. At airports, technology can help us make our facility more efficient and safer, but these infrastructure issues are not the only important factor. In the end we also have to make people happier. We try to encourage everyone—from check-in staff to immigration officers—to smile, be pleasant and treat people better, so the airport shifts from being an infrastructure business to a service business.

Ultimately, I believe that at Hong Kong International Airport we are selling an experience; a unique, enjoyable, memorable airport experience that you cannot find anywhere else in the world. Experience is not just about technology and infrastructure, it is a feeling. You cannot just use your head—as the airport operator, we have to use our heart to feel what our customers really want to feel, what makes a good experience for them.

This is the other side of the story when we talk about technology. Strictly speaking, technology does not have high value unless you can convert it into functionality—and that conversion takes innovation. Functionality itself does not give you full value either, unless you can deliver it in such a way that customers appreciate it. Appreciation is the true test: if they are not prepared to pay, and pay at a premium over similar types of products, then it has little value. Ultimately, we want to convert everything into an experience about which people feel great.

This is why we constantly conduct surveys and try to understand our customers' needs and how those needs are changing. In particular, we try to segment the market and not generalise about customers. We serve people from Hong Kong, but also a growing number of customers from Mainland

China—and what they want may be different. Similarly, business travellers and those coming for a vacation have different needs. So our aim is to segment the market and then differentiate our products. Some passengers may want high-quality service from their airlines and will be willing to pay for it; others may be more sensitive to price and will go with low-fare carriers. Similarly, we know that passengers have different shopping needs when they are at the airport, from top-of-the-range clothing stores to news outlets.

I believe that we are making good progress in meeting our customers' needs. Indeed, in an industry survey published in March 2005, Skytrax ranked us Best Airport Worldwide for the fifth consecutive year, based on business and leisure traveller feedback. Similarly AETRA, which is a joint collaboration between the airline association IATA and ACI, the airport association, awarded us 13 gold medals out of 31 categories last year, more than any other airport in the world, making us the World's Best Airport. But we have to continue making progress in this way, and to do so we need to keep in mind the true nature of the airport business. It is not just about infrastructure, technology or communications; it is about combining all of them to fulfill our role as an integrator who enhances the flow.

About Airport Authority Hong Kong

Hong Kong International Airport is the world's fifth busiest international passenger airport and the most active worldwide air cargo operation. Situated at the southern tip of China, within a fast growing economic region, the Airport connects its continuously expanding home market with the rest of the world. Some 60 scheduled passenger carriers and 17 all-cargo airlines operate 700 flights a day to 144 locations worldwide, including 42 in the Mainland of China. Hong Kong is one of the world's most successful airports and demonstrates the benefits that can be achieved through adopting and integrating emerging technologies with a focused customer service commitment.

2.1

Building an airport city

Pierre Graff | President and CEO, Aéroports de Paris, France

Airports have traditionally focused on their core operational activities, managing passengers and cargo and providing basic services while passengers wait for their flights. But that approach is beginning to change, especially in Europe, and many airports, including Aéroports de Paris (ADP), are looking to expand their range of services and build a new business model. ADP is in the process of being partially privatised, and while the French government will remain the majority owner, with at least 51 per cent of the shares, the new structure will allow it to make fundamental changes to the way it conducts business.

In the past, governments have tended to protect their national airlines. While private shareholders who invest in airports want to secure a return on their investment, economic viability is the key issue. So, alongside ADP's plans to improve core activities, it is focusing aggressively on connected activities such as retail, promotions and even real estate. Its ultimate vision is of a 'multi-services airport', integrated into its environment, that offers all the services people might need as they prepare to take a flight.

Aéroports de Paris comprises three airports: Paris-Charles-de-Gaulle, Paris-Orly and Le Bourget—less well known but the first European airport for business aviation. Last year the organisation handled 75.3 million passengers —the equivalent of around 200,000 people every day.

ADP is the second busiest airport in Europe behind London. In fact, Charles-de-Gaulle alone is the same size as Frankfurt Airport in Germany. There are 438 companies attached to the airport—the Air France-KLM group is the dominant partner, representing more than half of our traffic, but the other operations vary widely from airlines to cleaning contractors and engineering companies. That amounts to 100,000 people working in our airports. If you take into account people who work indirectly for us, some 300,000 people and their families live off the revenues from our activities.

All of this brings a number of challenges. In our core business we face significant issues balancing the needs of our different stakeholders. We have long-term obligations every time we upgrade our infrastructure at an airline's request. For example, if we upgrade a terminal, the airline's needs may have changed by the time we've built it, leaving us with the overhead. Similarly, we have a number of hurdles to overcome in terms of managing security and mitigating the environmental impact of airline activity. Technology will play an

important role in helping us achieve our objectives and our responsibilities. And as we look to expand our connected services and build our 'multi-services airport', we will encounter further issues. Every airport is a partial monopoly, so there is an inherent tension between the demands of the regulators, our obligations to our partners and customers and our desire to become profitable.

Building a profitable 'multi-services airport'

While our core business is welcoming companies and passengers who use our airports, it is possible to increase revenue through a wide range of activities connected to the main operations. For example, we are in the heart of Paris, which is renowned worldwide for the quality of its retail outlets, yet we struggle to find sufficient floor space for these outlets at ADP and, currently, we do not have the right mix of stores to suit the demographics and price ranges of our customers. Similarly, we have a significant amount of land capacity, where we can expand promotional activities for customers, such as advertising, or even develop real estate.

2.2

Potentially, this presents a huge opportunity for us to build a business model that delivers high-quality services whilst being profitable. All the main European airports are looking to take the same approach and step-by-step, year-after-year, you can see the beginnings of a global model appearing; for example, at Heathrow, Paris, Frankfurt, Amsterdam and, to an extent, Milan. Each of these airports has unique challenges and opportunities, but the economic model is fundamentally the same.

To achieve our goal we need to have imagination—we need new ideas that allow us to build greater synergy between the core business and all other services. To that end, we continually conduct surveys on our clients' and passengers' needs. Of course, they all want their aeroplanes to be on time, and they want to be less inconvenienced by security controls. But the big issue is, what do they want beyond that? Good, comfortable seats while they are waiting? High-quality shops selling at a competitive price? Perhaps space to be quiet and work—somewhere they can use their mobile phones, computers and wireless networks? Television for entertainment and information? In many cases, we know that frequent fliers are prepared to pay for VIP treatment but simply cannot find it.

Some of the solutions we will provide will be free and some will have a charge attached. This is the approach that Amsterdam's Schiphol Airport has taken—it has developed the concept of the 'airport city', a place where people and goods pass through, but where visitors can also find the kinds of activities and services that are available in a city.

The same kinds of developments are taking place in the Far East and Middle East, although not yet in America. We have one significant advantage over the US in that our major airlines, such as Air France-KLM, British Airways and Lufthansa, are in better financial shape than some of the major American carriers, and our prosperity rests to a large extent on the significant, constant demand that they serve. In addition, US airports are state or city-owned, while across Europe, governments such as ours are partially privatising their airports, turning them into normal businesses with commercial management. That gives the airports enormous freedom to pursue profits.

Challenges facing partial monopolies

At the same time, however, our model at ADP throws out its own challenges, not least because we operate a partial monopoly. The airlines need us—and we of course need them—and so we are obliged to work out deals with one another. But it is not always so easy to do. The airlines ask us to implement policies to deliver what they need: equipment, large terminals, good services, reliability and security, but we need to be paid for it. Generally speaking, that means increasing our fees while being cost-efficient. For airlines operating on thin margins, this can be a problem.

In some cases, airlines do have an element of choice that they can use in negotiating with us. If you are going from Toulouse to Moscow, for example, it makes little difference whether you change aircraft in Paris or Frankfurt, thus creating a certain level of competition between hub systems. But passengers going from Marseilles to Paris have no choice—they must land at our airport because we have a natural monopoly. That concerns the airlines.

As a result, we end up with structural conflicts. Some parts of our airport business are open to the free market and we can let the market set prices; but there is also a core part of the business where, because of this natural monopoly, we have an independent authority that regulates our activity. And it is here that most of the conflicts between the airlines and the airport emerge.

This is a classic problem for governments around the world, and there are various ways to solve it. Historically, the French Government instructed the airport to provide services as cheaply as possible, because the airlines were struggling commercially and took priority. But as soon as you bring in private shareholders this is no longer acceptable because it generates no return on the capital invested—it is a political approach, not a business approach. We are now following the lead of the British Government, which takes a very intelligent approach to regulating the British Airports Authority. It recognises that if you want to have private money in your airport, you must give visibility to your shareholders.

The best way to do this is to strike an agreement between the airport, the government and the regulatory authority while consulting infrastructure users and specifying how fees can be changed during a set period. It may take a year or so to reach agreement on how these fees are set—and in extreme cases the authorities may have to impose a settlement—but in the end you have an economical approach to which all parties agree.

Managing infrastructure challenges

Our ambition is not to become bigger than London, but to become a best practice model in certain domains, such as quality of service. This is not always easy to achieve, partly because the aviation industry evolves so quickly.

Air France recently advised ADP that it plans to buy several Boeing 777s. These aeroplanes need thicker runways, so we will need to make a major investment to cater for them. The main difficulty we face in these cases is that we generally have to invest for a long period, while the airlines invest for shorter periods and change their strategies relatively quickly. If they buy an aircraft and ask us to reconfigure our terminal, they might then sell the plane —but we may still be paying for that large investment.

2.2

While our core business is welcoming companies and passengers who use our airports, it is possible to increase revenue through a wide range of activities connected to the main operations. This presents a huge opportunity for us to build a business model that delivers high-quality services whilst being profitable.

The upside for us is that the volume of air traffic is increasing. It is not always easy to forecast growth, but expert opinion suggests that traffic will increase by 3 to 4 per cent annually up to 2020. So we are in an industry that is growing; our challenge is to keep up with the pace of change.

Around 15 years ago nobody in France, or indeed the rest of Europe, was talking about hubs. The model that had evolved was point-to-point links, and we built terminals that were designed for that approach. Today, however, the only way for big airlines to survive is to establish a hub strategy, so we have to build facilities and systems capable of dealing with them.

This is very costly and not the most efficient economic model. In a hub, many planes leave at the same time during peak hours, which means we have to invest in capacity to meet that highest level of need, rather than maximising capacity throughout the day. It also means that we have had to reorganise our terminals from the traditional point-to-point model. A passenger arriving on an aeroplane from Marseilles must be able to board his next plane 30 minutes later, with his baggage following; so we need short connections and all kinds of amenities that were not foreseen in our previous setup. This requires significant investment, and again it creates problems with fees—but it is a challenge that we have to meet in order to accompany our partners in their successful strategy.

But for the next 10 years or so I believe the hub model will remain very much as it operates today. It may change in 20 to 30 years, especially if we have new aircraft that are capable of going from Europe to America very cheaply on a point-to-point basis. But in the meantime, we will continue to see large demand for air transport, including fast-growing markets such as China or India. Hubs will be the only way to meet this demand because it is impossible to organise links between every point in the world.

We can already predict where the hubs will be in North America and the larger European cities, but it is not so clear in the Near East and Far East, where there is competition between Singapore, Bangkok, Hong Kong, Shanghai, Beijing and so on. Whichever cities emerge as aviation centres, it is clear that the larger international airports will adopt the kinds of economic model that I have described, because there will be limits on the amount of public money that is available to them.

This growth will be accompanied by more open sky agreements. Traffic rights are free within Europe and North America today, but not completely free between those two continents. Likewise, there are traffic restrictions between France and places such as Sierra Leone or Egypt. I think that in 10 to 15 years' time the legal situation will be very different. We will have more open sky agreements and even open space areas—not necessarily between individual states, but perhaps between different areas, with parts of North America striking agreements with certain areas in Europe or the Far East.

Technology: great expectations

For some reason, passengers associate airports with modern technology far more than other forms of transport and expect access to newer technology when they travel by aeroplane. Take the underground railway system; it is very complex to build and run, yet passengers do not expect Wi-Fi services when they use it. However, they do expect such services when they come through an airport.

Airports are very complex organisations and many activities are already automated, with central computer systems and extensive information and communications networks. But there are two areas where I believe we will see significant improvements in the use of technology in coming years.

The first is security. Since September 11th, security has become a major issue for the air transport industry, and while we already make extensive use of equipment to detect weapons and explosives, we are dealing with people with very creative imaginations, so we need to enhance our response continually. We need a system capable of scanning baggage very quickly, for example, as well as rapid ways of reading biometrics. We are making progress, but it is not fast enough, and systems could be much less expensive and more efficient.

In Paris we have started to experiment with a number of new systems. We are testing one that traces explosives on clothes, and while it is still at an experimental stage, if it works well we may be able to apply it more widely. One problem we face is that this kind of technology is rare and it changes very quickly, so it is not always easy for us to decide which kind of equipment we should buy. If we invest in something, we have to ask whether it will be obsolete in one or two years' time: alternatively, we may find ourselves experimenting with technology that is not totally reliable today, but might be much more efficient in a couple of years' time. These are not simple decisions.

2.2

For some reason, passengers associate airports with modern technology far more than other forms of transport and expect access to newer technology when they travel by aeroplane.

The second area where we need to see progress is in tackling environmental problems. This is a major concern for us: while we can build a great economic model for the airport, we also need to take account of our surroundings and do our best to ensure that people living near the airport do not have to tolerate excessive noise and pollution. This is a difficult issue and there is no simple answer. With trains and cars you can modify engines and build walls around houses to block some of the noise, but there is no easy technological solution for aircraft. It is possible to take steps to reduce the noise of the engines, but that ultimately increases the amount of greenhouse gases generated. All airports are making some progress in this respect, but there is much more to be done by the aeronautical industry.

The future

Looking to the future, one area that is difficult to predict is whether low-cost carriers can continue to grow as quickly as they have until now. For one thing, the differences between their model and the traditional airlines will diminish as the larger carriers will be forced to improve their productivity and copy some of their ideas. At the same time, the low-cost carriers have to pay their pilots and other employees competitive rates and pay the same fees and charges as everyone else.

There will still be a market for the low-cost carriers, but it is important to distinguish between the two different types. When you operate in a market with large competitors you have two options: you can either struggle on head-to-head with your competitors, or you accept that the market contains too many strong players and you focus elsewhere. Some low-cost carriers focus on attracting customers who travel with the big companies today—so they will continue to fly into the big airports, and will hope to win through better productivity.

The other kind of carrier—which includes organisations such as Ryan Air—tries to attract passengers who do not typically travel by plane, and avoids competition with the larger companies by offering short links and efficient point-to-point services from secondary airports that do not require hubs and huge infrastructure. I think this second group will remain in business, and as a result, there will be a place for smaller, simple airports specialising in providing equipment for them. Those smaller airports may, of course, be owned by large airports—just as Frankfurt Hahn airport is in Germany.

In the past, our Government's priority was the health of the airlines, and it is only recently that they have become interested in the economic model of the airport.

Our airport needs to be involved from the very beginning to deal with all the change that continues to affect the travel industry, working to develop new initiatives and take advantage of technological innovation to meet the demands of airlines and passengers. In many respects it is a marketing job, and it seems to me that in the old days the industry in general did not develop sufficient marketing expertise.

In the past, our Government's priority was the health of the airlines, and it is only recently that they have become interested in the economic model of the airport as we start to attract private investors. It is only natural, therefore, that we should now be starting to focus on the exciting possibilities open to us—ways to redress conflicts of interest with the airlines over fees, improve services for passengers and turn the concept of the 'airport city' into reality.

About Aéroports de Paris

ADP is Europe's second largest airport authority and the sixth largest worldwide, with 2004 revenues of over €1.8 billion and 75.3 million passengers.

ADP comprises three complementary airport platforms:
Charles DeGaulle, the most powerful hub in Europe; Orly, a convenient airport for passengers and a user-friendly airport for the airlines, and Le Bourget, the European leader in business aviation.

2.2

Customer-centric operations: key to success

Chua Kee Thiam | Head of Information Technology,
PSA Singapore Terminals, Singapore

As with any business, our most important partnership is with our customers—we have to work closely with them to understand their needs, and by doing so we can start to offer the kinds of value-added services they are looking for. Our main focus, therefore, is to continually improve the efficiency of our customer-facing operations and back-end services, and enhance the quality of the value-added services we provide.

PSA Singapore Terminals is the world's largest container transhipment hub. Its four container terminals at Tanjong Pagar, Keppel, Brani and Pasir Panjang operate as one seamless and integrated facility. Two hundred of the world's shipping lines call at PSA Singapore Terminals, offering connections to 600 ports in 123 countries. This includes daily sailings to every major port in the world. In 2004, PSA Singapore Terminals handled 20.6 million Twenty-foot Equivalent Units (TEUs) of containers in 2004. Such high volumes of containers require a combination of modern physical infrastructure and advanced information management, and much of our success relies on the systems that we have built.

Managing front- and back-end services

PSA's strength lies in our ability to handle large-scale, complex transhipment arrangements efficiently and meet customers' needs in their hubbing operations. PSA Singapore Terminals' operational and administrative functions are underpinned by two core systems that use some of the most advanced technology in the shipping world today: PORTNET®, which handles the business-to-business transactions and workflow with the customers, and CITOS®, the enterprise resource planning system that commands and controls highly complex transhipment operations. These systems provide the critical infrastructure for all of our port services.

PORTNET® was set up in 1984, and has been through several iterations; it started off as a mainframe-based system, and was subsequently rebuilt in a Unix environment. It is now being upgraded to take advantage of Java and the Internet. Today it handles 90 million transactions annually with 7,500 users connected to it, ranging from shipping lines, transportation companies and truckers, to government agencies such as Immigration and Checkpoints Authority and the Maritime and Port Authority of Singapore. As the world's first business-to-business shipping e-community, PORTNET® has the participation of the entire port and shipping community that operates in Singapore.

At one level, PORTNET® can be thought of as a documentation gateway with in-built workflows that provides 100 per cent paperless transactions— in effect, it is the hub that facilitates the entire flow through the port and shipping community. What that means in practice is that, by running one central system, we eliminate all the duplication that would otherwise take place whenever suppliers and customers have to maintain numerous different systems.

From an operational perspective, our aim is to provide services that help customers streamline their shipments, making them more efficient and in turn bringing more volume into Singapore. On top of that, PORTNET® also provides a platform for value-added solutions.

2.3

Such high volumes of containers require a combination of modern physical infrastructure and advanced information management, and much of our success relies on the systems that we have built.

If we look at the management of slot space, for example, most shipping lines share slots, just as airlines co-share at airports. They need to keep track of how effectively they utilise them, whether they overbook or underbook them. This would normally be actioned by the customer, but at Singapore it is one of the services we provide through PORTNET®. Similarly, we offer transhipment management systems, which help customers automate their transhipment operations in Singapore seamlessly.

Much of the back-office paperwork associated with port management has also been automated, in order to reduce both our own and our customers' manual processes. We make extensive use of Electronic Data Interchange (EDI), which has been adopted as standard by the shipping lines and most ports, and provides a common format to send and match electronic invoices. In some cases it has been possible to build in additional services to help companies automatically match invoices against their internal purchase order numbers. We also provide extensive management reporting to our customers for decision-making and planning.

CITOS®, which runs alongside PORTNET®, is a large and complex system developed specifically to help us manage complex container transhipment operations. Over time, large parts of our back-end operations have been automated and optimised through this system. For example, our award-winning, paperless Flow-Through Gate system uses multiple image-capturing and number recognition technologies. CITOS® and PORTNET® are closely integrated through very fast gateways, providing an end-to-end infrastructure that supports our different services. As a result of that integration, we can clear one truck in approximately 25 seconds through paperless gate processing, compared to the two minutes it used to take before the system was implemented. It has also been possible to reduce the number of people within the processing cycle—it used to require one person per lane, but now each employee controls seven lanes. This kind of improvement is critical to our business. Singapore is very small and the port is close to the central business district, so the manner in which traffic flows into and out of the port has a significant impact both on the quality of service we offer and on the wider community.

Wireless and tracking technologies

Alongside these two core systems we have adopted a number of other technologies in recent years, in many cases as one of the earliest adopters. Extensive investment has been made in wireless connectivity. In fact, many years ago, PSA implemented a proprietary wireless narrowband system together with wireless LAN in its terminals to cover all truck- and container-handling crane movements. The emergence of public systems using General Packet Radio Service means that we will no longer be restricted by location and will be able to take this infrastructure to a new level.

In fact, the network as a whole is becoming increasingly important, and we need to be able to take advantage of both voice and video processing, particularly where it can generate images of containers on screen for our operators to handle. The technology is not yet mature, and the network bandwidth is not available presently, but this is something PSA will continue to watch going forward.

Tracking is also critical to PSA's operations and it presents a number of challenges. Most people's experience with this kind of technology is based on their use of track and trace systems from delivery companies, but they tend to forget the important fact that the delivery company controls every part of that process, so it has been able to develop its own end-to-end system. Tracking and tracing containers, however, is not the exclusive domain of one port—we are only one node in the overall process. So our work needs to contribute to a broader process.

Fortunately, Singapore does not experience the difficulties faced by some other ports in tracking containers on the ground. At PSA Singapore Terminals, we know the exact location of each container at any one time—in fact, transponders have been used at the container stacking yard since the technology first emerged, and it is still used to identify locations and track movements. From the point that they are offloaded onto the dock to the time they arrive at the terminals, the exact location of each container is known. We may be handling millions of containers, but we seldom lose sight of any one of them.

The network as a whole is becoming increasingly important and we need to be able to take advantage of both voice and video processing.

Similarly, PSA Singapore Terminals has been using Radio Frequency Identification (RFID) since the mid-1990s to track container trucks. Like many other early adopters, the problem we have experienced in the past has been the lack of standards; it presents similar challenges to barcoding, where a specific manufacturer's device has to be purchased to read their own codes. Standards are now evolving, of course, and as our partners and customers start to employ RFID more widely, we will continue to use this technology both from a logistical point of view and to improve security.

2.3

All of our own trucks are also fitted with Global Positioning Systems, managed through our Prime Mover Tracking System, which enables us to know exactly where each one is physically located and also where it fits into the overall logistics process. Currently, we cannot track external trucks, so we rely on pre-notification from our partners using EDI. Combined with our ability to track and manage early and late-running ships, this means we have all of the logistical information needed to handle the logistics process efficiently.

Challenges

As part of our strategy to sustain long-term growth and maintain Singapore's premier status as the world's largest transhipment hub, PSA is adding 15 new berths at Pasir Panjang Terminal by 2011. These new berths will boost PSA's annual handling capacity in Singapore from 20 million TEUs to 31 million TEUs. Three new berths at Pasir Panjang Terminal came into operation between June and August 2005. The new berths, with a maximum draft of up to 16 metres, are equipped with new super post-Panamax quay cranes that are capable of handling mega containerships with capacity in excess of 8,000 TEUs. PSA has already invested more than S$400 million on new port equipment and technology for these new berths.

Of course, the larger the ships, the more goods they can carry, and the challenge will be to handle loading and discharging operations more efficiently. Improvements will have to be made in IT, port engineering technology and work processes, particularly in the use of cranes with multi-lift capabilities. Singapore must be able to cater for these new ways of working and continually upgrade its facilities.

Similarly, we continually try to deliver efficiencies in terms of the way we use yard space. As more ships come in and the volume of containers increases, we require more space and have to optimise the way we work. That means we must look at multiple types of automation and also take greater advantage of mobile technologies and new optimisation techniques. This technology will change the way the port is managed; most ports today operate through central control, but in the future, mobility would allow them to have more flexible management.

The Government actually serves as a catalyst for the adoption of new technologies by encouraging stakeholders to adopt solutions.

We have made similar productivity improvements with yard cranes, which are now managed remotely at Pasir Panjang Terminal. Previously, it needed one operator in each crane; today, the operator sits inside an air-conditioned control room, and one person can now handle up to half a dozen cranes.

Security

The events of 9/11 had an impact on PSA as they did for so many other businesses around the world. Today there is a far greater emphasis not just on security, but on the concept of continuous security as well. There are many initiatives to improve the security of containers, and as a major hub port, we participate in whatever way we can to get ourselves ready. Security authorities have implemented Gamma Ray Scanning for selected international and local containers, for example. It is important to ensure that these additional measures that are deployed at our terminals do not impact on our efficiency, so we liaise very closely with organisations such as Singapore's Immigration and Checkpoints Authority. Many initiatives are underway, including Operation Safe Commerce by the US Department of Homeland Security.

Having said that, I do not believe security is simply the role of the ports. Checking should start at the source, at the point where the container is packed; it then needs to be secured at every point along the flow to ensure it is not tampered with. A wide range of technologies is used to achieve this; some advocate the use of electronics, while others prefer to rely on track and trace to locate where the container is throughout its journey. But either way, a worldwide effort is needed to make this happen.

Looking forward

Information will continue to be critical to our ability to provide value-added services, and in the future we will be looking to improve the way we integrate with our partners and exchange information in new ways that go beyond EDI. One important player in that process will be the support of the Singapore Government in any new IT initiative. PSA and the authorities cooperate closely—for example, with Customs to facilitate container inspections. This helps to make our overall operations very efficient for the whole port community.

The Government actually serves as a catalyst for the adoption of new technologies by encouraging stakeholders to adopt solutions, and also acts as a facilitator to assist in the efficiency of the process flow. Any processing done electronically requires government support—in order for PSA to send invoices electronically to our customers, for example, it is essential we have the backing of the tax authorities.

If we can work closely with all of the players involved—our partners, our customers and the authorities—I believe that we will be able to extend our existing physical and electronic infrastructure to handle the growth in shipping volumes that we project for the coming years.

About PSA Singapore Terminals

PSA Singapore Terminals is the world's largest container transhipment hub. As the 'World's Port of Call', PSA Singapore Terminals links shippers to an excellent network of 200 shipping lines with connections to 600 ports in 123 countries. Shippers have access to daily sailings to every major port in the world at this mega-hub. Its position as a standard-bearer of excellence in port operations has consistently been recognised by the shipping community. It was voted the 'Best Container Terminal Operator (Asia)' for the 16th time at the 2005 Asian Freight & Supply Chain Awards, and 'Best Container Terminal Operator' at the Lloyd's List Maritime Asia Awards 2005 for the sixth time since its inauguration in 1999. In 2004, PSA Singapore Terminals handled 20.6 million TEUs.

2.3

Managing growth at New York's airports

Bill DeCota | Director of Aviation, The Port Authority of New York and New Jersey, U.S.

Like any organization of its kind and size, the Port Authority of New York and New Jersey (PANYNJ) faces a number of challenges. Fortunately there is a range of solutions, many of them technology-based. What is clear is that many of the old solutions are no longer applicable. It used to be the case that if you ran out of space, you built a new terminal. That no longer works.

Instead, we need to harness technology to make more of the space we already have, whether we talk about baggage handling, bigger aircraft, air traffic control, or any other of the challenges we face. This is made harder by issues such as changing travel patterns—for example, growth in the number of smaller planes carrying fewer people.

At the same time, we want to move forward and improve the quality of service for our customers, the traveling public. That means making institutional changes as well as altering processes. All that said, airports are profitable—and long may they remain so.

Challenges and solutions

This is one of the largest airport systems in the world. Newark Liberty, Kennedy, and LaGuardia combined handled 94 million passengers this year, which is 10 million more than we catered to the year before, and we are projecting that it will rise to 100 million passengers per year by the end of 2005. We also handle nearly three million tons of cargo per year and our projections are that this will grow robustly over the next 10 years. And we do all of this in a confined space—just 8,500 acres including Teterboro Airport, our general aviation airport. To put this in context, we currently handle 1.4 million planes per year, which means that during most of the day, a plane lands or takes off at one of our airports every 30 seconds.

Like the airline industry, we face a number of major challenges. Capacity is a significant problem because we simply do not have the space to build extra facilities to accomodate growth. The emergence of new aircraft like the A380 and the growing popularity of smaller regional jets are changing the shape of the industry. We have ongoing tensions between the financial needs of the airlines and our desire to improve continually the quality of service provided to passengers. We also operate in a highly regulated environment that makes it difficult to address some of the inefficiencies inherent in the way the relationship between airports and airlines is structured.

But we also have a number of potential solutions, many of them rooted in technology. New technologies will potentially touch every aspect of the business, from the way passengers check in for their flights to the way we manage planes in the air. The approach to meeting the growing demand for air capacity is to harness some of these technologies, and to take bold steps to tackle some of the fundamental infrastructure and political issues.

Capacity, technology, and bricks and mortar

Airports are nothing more than a physical infrastructure—pavement, terminals, cargo buildings, fueling systems, and so forth—but they team up with another form of technology in the shape of aircraft. For years, as that technology got faster and bigger and traveled farther distances, we were able to keep pace with demand by extending our runways and building international terminals. Newark was one of the first airports to have modern air traffic control technology; they flashed green lights from the tower if it was okay to land and a red light if a plane was to go back around.

2.4

> We need to harness technology to make more of the space we already have, whether we talk about baggage handling, bigger aircraft, air traffic control, or many other of the challenges we face.

Looking back, to some extent we were lucky to be able to keep up with demand. On the wall in my office I have a wonderful report from the late 1920s by the chief engineer of the then Port of New York Authority. It was about the need for an "aeroport," as it was described, in the New York metropolitan region. It is interesting because we were visionary enough to recognize the technology potential, but we did not look far enough ahead to realize how the technology would evolve. The report says the ideal "aeroport" needed 250 acres with a 1,000-foot runway. Today, Denver airport is 33,000 acres, Dallas Fort Worth is 18,000 acres, Dulles Airport is 10,000 acres, and Kennedy has a runway of 14,400 feet. Our smallest airport, LaGuardia, is 780 acres and it somehow manages to handle 24 million passengers, which is extremely unusual.

Today there is no more room for additional bricks and mortar, and that is the biggest challenge. How can we grow an airport system from 94 million per year passengers today to 126 million passengers per year by 2015? How can we take an airport system that now handles three million tons of cargo per year, and handle four and a half million tons of cargo by the year 2015? Building another runway or some other major capital construction project is not the answer; the answer is technology.

That means improved air traffic control, bigger and different types of aircraft technology, and new technologies to manage the airport infrastructure.

As far as air traffic control is concerned, using radio beacons on the ground in order to navigate aircraft does not make sense. There are constellations of satellites circumnavigating the earth that are very capable of global positioning in perfect triangulation, and they are enhanced by another system called the wide area augmentation system.

With the right flight management systems inside the aircraft, you can get away from traditional notions of air traffic control and introduce free flight, where we meander through the air. There is a wonderful potential to increase the air space beyond where it is today. The physics are not going to change with regard to aircraft technology: planes are still going to land on the ground and people will still be going to a boarding gate 20 or 30 years from now. But while the air space itself is still finite, we can make much more efficient use of it.

The same is true of the aircraft themselves. With the A380 super-jumbo, we will be able to get 555 people and thousands of tons of cargo onto a plane. That will make a big difference in terms of capacity. One secret to flying bigger planes is being able to use existing runways that are 150 feet wide instead of 200 feet wide, because those planes are capable of such precise navigation that all you have to worry about is how you maneuver them on the ground. Putting more people in the plane means fewer movements both on the ground and in the air, so suddenly I may be able to expand capacity without increasing my 1.4 million aircraft movements.

The impact of these new aircraft could be felt widely across the industry. When the Boeing 747 came to New York in 1971, one unexpected consequence was that the entire fleet upgauged, and I think the same thing is going to happen with the A380. A few A380 flights are not going to make the difference; rather, the important issue is that the whole fleet seems to upgauge and the smaller planes fall off the bottom of the mix.

Capacity versus freedom of choice

The flipside of these developments at the high-end is the rapid growth of regional jets, with 50-seat planes now commonly flying multiple times to small destinations. If you have 15 flights a day to Richmond, Virginia on a 50-seat plane, it is clearly not conducive to maximizing airport capacity. Worse, while older propeller planes traveled at a different altitude and followed different flight patterns than jumbo jets, these regional jets travel in exactly the same pattern, and it is creating a significant problem for us.

This is not a commercial issue, it is an operational issue. Ultimately, choice and capacity are not synonymous, and we believe there will either have to be new pricing regulations or new administrative rulings.

Today landing at an airport is like using a public utility. Whether we live in Nebraska or New York, we pay an average cost to gain access to the telephone network and to pay for the overall cost of producing the telephone poles and the lines—and that is what happens at the airfield. LaGuardia may have the most highly demanded airside resource anywhere in the world— but you pay the average weight-based cost to land there. So inevitably oversubscription results, and a lot of people fly on 50-seat planes.

There is a wonderful potential to increase the air space beyond where it is today.

One option is to charge people for the privilege of flying on smaller planes. The problem is that LaGuardia is their airport of choice because it is so convenient to Manhattan, which is where wealthy business people with their own private jets want to go. Politically, it is hard to chase an extremely wealthy, well-heeled opinion maker out of that slot at LaGuardia, and it is hard, too, to discourage them by using price. If someone has spent US$40 million on a Boeing business jet with his or her name on it, an increase in landing fees of a thousand dollars is a small deterrent.

2.4

Planes landing at LaGuardia airport typically have on average of 68 passengers. Even at Kennedy there are only 104 passengers on average. So we have to work on improving efficiency and, while we can create some extra capacity through technology, some of it has to come through policy and regulation.

Modernizing infrastructure

There are also a number of things we can change to improve airport infrastructure. In Europe, for example, airports have control of ground level, pushing back aircraft and carrying out other duties, and the U.S. should follow suit. Today, third parties do that or the airlines do it for themselves.

Similarly, we need common information displays. Today, you go into an airport and find information displays specific to airlines, whereas a common feed, where flight information is displayed in one place, makes more sense. There is some resistance to this kind of centralized control from airlines with sophisticated check-in and display systems, who believe they would lose competitive advantage if everything were standardized. But we have 135 airlines operating at one airport, all with different views as to how they are going to compete with each other. My job ultimately is to try to prevail over that situation and bring some order and direction to it.

By the same token, "common use" terminals, are more efficient than separate terminals, where one airline has exclusive use. We already have some common use facilities such as Terminal B at Newark and the international arrivals building at Kennedy Airport, and as we develop the infrastructure this is something we aim to expand.

For example, we are building a new US$875 million terminal at Kennedy Airport, and are ensuring it is built on a common infrastructure to accommodate any kind of aircraft that wants to operate there. Airline leases will have strong utilization provisions. For example, if the number of daily seats sold by an airline falls below the standard specified in the lease, we can release gates to other carriers.

From a passenger perspective, the changes will be both practical and radical. Air travel today is very linear. If you want to fly from New York to Tokyo, you make a reservation, call the car company to take you to the airport, check in, go through security, shop at the duty free store for your favorite wine, and finally board the aircraft. But if any link in the chain breaks, it creates problems for you.

We are working on a concept called Easy Travel (E-Z), which puts you at the center of your own travel universe. Whether you are on your laptop, at work on your desktop machine, using a wireless device, or an airport kiosk, every element of your trip is managed and you are identified and known at each stage. The fact that we have wireless technology and extremely small devices that not only have memories but can also communicate with one another is an incredible breakthrough that will have massive implications for capacity, service, and security at airports.

Think of developments such as e-ticketing and automated check-in, or Radio Frequency Identification (RFID) on your baggage tag that ensures it can be tracked at all times. Your duty free items could be brought to you automatically. If you drive to the airport, an E-Z Pass tag pays for your parking and can reserve a spot for you. And consider the whole idea of the Trusted Traveler, which allows you to be identified and fast-tracked through security if you are willing to submit yourself to a background check. This means the airport need not worry about picking through every person heading for the gates.

Similarly, using shared technology means it also becomes more flexible. If airline XYZ goes out of business, ABC can walk up and plug its computer in instead. Airlines will no longer need to have their own specific baggage belt, which frustrates passengers who see one running empty when another is completely backed up; instead, everything is used to maximum efficiency.

This has big implications for capacity. Back in 2000, we would have said there are going to be x many customers, so we will put in y many ticket counters. Now the need for that many ticket counters has fallen because most people are using e-tickets. Likewise, baggage scanners used to occupy huge amounts of space, while the latest systems can sit on top of counters. We also have in-line baggage screening, which automatically takes the bag, decides whether there is a problem, does a secondary scan, and ultimately can focus down to just a couple of bags.

The fact that we have wireless technology and extremely small devices that not only have memories but can also communicate with one another is an incredible breakthrough that will have massive implications for capacity, service, and security.

Technology like this is going to revolutionize airline capacity. You can take 8,500 acres of property and very little bricks and mortar, and begin to use technology in a way that accommodates the future.

2.4

It is important to point out that much of this lies beyond the scope of individual airports. For one thing, technology is so expensive that you cannot develop this application for one airport—the cost needs to be spread. More importantly, while these systems do have limited utility in terms of customer service at an individual airport, you need similar infrastructure at either end because the airport systems need to communicate. Ultimately it has to become worldwide, or a new interoperability standard needs to be developed. That is the responsibility of either governments or industry associations like the International Air Transport Association.

Customer service and the peculiar dynamics of airports

Along with capacity issues, improving the quality of customer service is a top priority for us, but the unique nature of the airport industry presents some challenges.

To begin with, our customers are an extremely diverse group of people. Passengers with children are different from the elderly who may need assistance, who are different from single travelers going on one-day business trips. We are trying to facilitate the movement of these passengers through mass customization, taking the same basic product and putting a new shell around it to make it seem like something different. It is like trying to take Henry Ford's plain black Model T and call one the Ford Explorer, another the Lincoln Continental Sedan, and so forth. Each model meets different people's needs and desires and perhaps performs differently—one does off-road, one is better for cruising and touring—but at heart it is the same function. Airports exist to get people and cargo out of land vehicles and into air vehicles, and vice versa.

That sounds pretty simple, but in practice it is complicated. We know how to please our customers in our terminals and when they shop in our stores. We also know that in the cargo industry, the freight forwarders, container station operators, and cargo brokers are all part of our customer base. But the PANYNJ delivers this service in an extremely difficult environment because only 1,000 of the 72,000 people who work at our airports actually work directly for the Authority. So effectively, my job is to set standards for employees of other organizations to work by.

There is some indirect control on these third-party businesses, as the Authority controls whether or not they get leases and permits. And we can also set standards for all the services that the Port Authority itself delivers, such as parking. So I expect my parking lot cashiers to address you, speak clearly, not have loud music when you exit, and not have newspapers in the windows of the toll booth. Consistency is important, too; if there is a multilingual services representative at Kennedy Airport, there will be one at Newark Liberty and LaGuardia.

While airlines and airports have never disagreed over the fundamentals of quality, service, price, value, and variety, ultimately, there is tension between the two and conflict arises over the economics of delivering those fundamentals. The airline industry has been losing money for a long time, so it finds it hard to invest and does not want airports imposing standards that have associated costs. That creates tension between an airline that is trying to survive and an airport operator that believes its customer deserves a fine level of service, regardless of the financial condition of the industry, simply because the customer is paying.

Forging a new relationship with airlines

The way airlines and airports work together is that the airlines collect the majority of the revenues from the passenger and then pass a small percentage back to the airport operator. They have historically tried to resist passing on that revenue because they need every penny to try to balance their books. The airline industry lost US$9 billion in 2004—in fact, when you look at it, the industry has lost money since the advent of commercial aviation. So our problem is, how can we provide the infrastructure and services we need to offer, when our primary partner is not capable of supporting us financially?

Bear in mind that airports are highly regulated in terms of doing business, including the way they relate to airlines and set pricing. Constitutionally, no one can interfere with the smooth working of trade, so the U.S. Department of Transportation will not allow us to do certain things that would influence trade, travel, commerce, and tourism. We have to price our airport facilities to airlines on a fair and non-discriminatory basis, for example, and that has always been interpreted historically on a cost-based, weight-based landing fee. These rules limit the relationship an airport has with airlines and keep us in an old-fashioned type of business relationship.

What we need is a new definition of the airport/airline partnership. Currently, we charge people to park in our parking lot; we get a share of all food, beverage, and retail revenues at the airport; and we charge terminal rates and landing fees.

The most radical approach would be to scrap these charges altogether and give airlines absolutely free access to airports, allowing them to pick up passengers, charge whatever they want, and compete with each other on the level of service they provide. We could raise the same amount of money we get today by simply charging US$15 to every customer who comes in the door, whether they are arriving or departing, and charging cargo around US$100 a ton.

Many airports today operate with the airlines dictating their decisions, thanks to leases that allow them to veto capital investments at airports.

2.4

Not only would we have replaced our revenue, we would also be dealing directly with the end customer. We believe that customers are effectively paying this money today through the ticket price. The airports could charge what they want because, to an extent, the market would regulate it, and hopefully we would all be reasonable and charge based upon our true infrastructure requirements.

Many airports today operate with the airlines dictating their decisions, thanks to leases that allow them to veto capital investments at airports. Why are the airlines making those decisions? This is something we have to keep discussing with government—airports are a unit of government just like the federal government. We are here to protect the common good, not to make scarce profits and give them away.

The fact is that airports do make money—they have extremely high credit ratings and are very good for municipal credit. Airlines have had a hard time making money, but the hope is that the industry is re-adapting itself so that it can compete. We know that an airline such as Southwest can make money even at US$100 per ticket because it is extremely efficient. Had fuel prices not risen so high, many more airlines would be profitable today. There will be some losses, some will not survive—but the fact is that there are still 700 million people who want to fly, and who need both the airport infrastructure and the airlines to do so.

I believe that airlines will be self-sustaining in the long run, fuelled by the huge growth for travel that looks set to continue for the foreseeable future. That convinces us that airports in general, and the PANYNJ in particular, are doing the right thing. With the right ideas coupled with the right technology and public support, we plan to continue forging ahead—with the airlines by our side.

About The Port Authority of New York and New Jersey
The Port Authority of New York and New Jersey manages and maintains the bridges, tunnels, bus terminals, airports, PATH rail system, and seaport that are critical to the bi-state region's trade and transportation capabilities. It also owns the 16-acre World Trade Center site. Through its facilities and services, people are able to make vital connections and businesses are able to grow.

Suppliers

Solutions for transportation communications

John Belcher | Chairman and CEO, ARINC Inc., U.S.

The transportation industry faces major challenges. The aviation industry alone is a huge driver for the United States economy—some 10 million jobs are tied to it—yet last year the airline sector lost US$5.5 billion, compounding a series of losses reported over previous years. The cost of oil, and therefore aviation fuel, a dominant cost driver for the airline industry, is rising; we have capacity problems in terms of runways and other infrastructure, and the regulatory environment is nowhere near as flexible and cost-effective as it could be. In some instances, regulatory issues have prevented the aviation industry from implementing measures that we know would improve efficiency and help the industry by cutting fuel costs.

There are similar problems elsewhere. The U.S. rail industry, for example, is hampered by infrastructure limitations that prevent it from building a high-speed train network. In the shipping sector, some 20 percent of the containers that move around the world are either untracked, become lost, or are difficult to find, presenting significant problems in terms of efficiency and security.

In many cases, the technology already exists to tackle these problems—the challenge we face is putting that technology to use. In some instances we need to wait for the regulatory environment to catch up—for example, as early as 1990 we began looking at the pico-cell technology that allows mobile phones to be used from aircraft, yet regulators have only recently begun to seriously consider approving this kind of service. In other cases we need to prove the commercial case for implementing the technology; in an industry where capital expenditure is so closely monitored, we need to demonstrate that technology improvements make a real difference in cutting operating costs.

One useful example of this is the ubiquity of common user systems available at airports for check-in. These had been widely used outside the United States because they make it more efficient for an airport to operate but, for a very long time, U.S. airlines were reluctant to bring them in because they thought using their own dedicated systems brought them competitive advantage.

Now that the airlines have started adopting common user systems, we are beginning to see the extension of these technologies to other areas. Hotels in Las Vegas were the first "pioneers" to consider putting in a common user kiosk in their lobbies so that customers could check in, get a boarding pass, and have their bags taken care of there and then. The business case for the hotel owner was that the patrons would stay another hour and carry on gambling—and it worked.

Other applications are also possible from the same common use platform. I have taken a few cruises and the thing I hate is that on the last night they take my bags, I get off the ship, and I find myself looking at thousands of pieces of luggage—I have no idea where mine is and I've got to catch a plane. In conjunction with partners, we have moved our kiosks to six major cruise lines that are prepared to use the system for air travel check in; that is, you hand over your luggage on the ship, they give you your boarding pass and bag tags, you go to the airport, and when you get there, your bags are already on the aircraft.

3.1

> With a combination of creative thinking, a commercial business case, and some reform of the regulatory environment, we can tackle many of the challenges that the transportation industry faces.

With a combination of creative thinking, a commercial business case, and some reform of the regulatory environment, we can tackle many of the challenges that the transportation industry faces.

Technology and regulatory challenges

The U.S. aviation industry faces significant technology challenges, particularly with air traffic control. Part of the problem is that, as an industry, we tend to develop very detailed specifications for individual systems, but it can take years to get through the design, approval, and build process. So by the time you deliver a system, you're doing it with 10-year-old technology. But there are lots of systems around the world that you can install off-the-shelf and modify to your own needs. I do think the industry should be more prepared to take what's already available and customize it to meet its core needs, rather than trying to design from the ground up.

We also have a significant problem handling the older, legacy systems in use for air traffic control. It was not hard for the airlines to implement new, high-speed air/ground data link systems to tie to their operational centers, but it has proved much harder for them to feed into and take data out of the Federal Aviation Administration (FAA), mainly because its legacy systems cannot handle the data. The FAA is currently upgrading all of its legacy air traffic control systems, but the first deliverables will not be in place until 2009.

Many other countries are using off-the-shelf air traffic control systems, so they can handle these kinds of changes in a matter of days. This is why we have been able to install a high-speed air VHF Digital Link Mode 2 (VDLM2) in Japan and parts of Europe. To be fair, the traffic systems are much more complex in the U.S. than some of these countries, but the legacy systems remain a significant impediment.

> If we were to privatize the FAA and move it one more step away from politics, it would be able to make more decisions on a commercial rather than political basis.

Alongside these technology issues, there are also a number of regulatory challenges. For example, we have installed VDL (VHF Data Link) Mode 2 into 180 U.S. sites, but the FAA is still deciding whether to go with VDL Mode 2, 3, or 4. Had they decided earlier, the system would already be in place and ready for use. We know it can increase the effectiveness and capacity of airspace—something that has been proven by the FAA's own studies—and it can provide huge benefits. For every minute you save on a global basis, you save billions of dollars in terms of fuel, labor costs, and so forth—and from an environmental perspective, you save having to burn hundreds of thousands of pounds of fuel.

I think the solution lies not in giving the FAA more money, but in changing the rules of engagement so that Congress allows the FAA to use the money it has more effectively. If we were to privatize the FAA and move it one more step away from politics, it would be able to make more decisions on a commercial rather than political basis; for example, determining aviation points of service based on a need versus political basis.

There are over 30 countries around the world that have privatized air navigation services and facilities, and they are all doing well. They reduced the costs to the airlines and there is no reason that model could not work in the U.S. and elsewhere.

A Canada-based consulting company I led a few years ago conducted a major study on all facets of aviation in Canada—from policy to technology, privatization and legislation—and we made 82 recommendations. Number one was to privatize Canada's air traffic control system. They did it, and NAV CANADA, the corporation that now owns and operates the civil air navigation service, has proved effective; in terms of headcount alone, they have reduced their employee numbers considerably.

I believe there is one core role for government, and that is legislation. Government handles the regulatory side to cover safety and security—but it should let industry run operations, based on market demand.

Building a commercial proposition

Overcoming these challenges is not just about regulations, of course—it is also about demonstrating the value that technology brings. If I cannot show an airline that, by using a particular technology, operating costs will quickly decrease, they will not look at it. One needs to go to an airline and say, "If you put this system in, it will reduce your block-to-block time by six minutes." That offers huge savings for airlines in terms of pilots, operators, and fuel.

There is a lot of technology available today that, in theory, could help solve some of our challenges, but it is a matter of commercializing it. Back in 1979 when communications between aircraft and the ground were exclusively voice driven, the concept of a digital link to aircraft called Air Ground Data Link was introduced. Before it was developed, the pilot would have to sign clearance papers from the cockpit—someone would literally have to walk up the aisle with the documents. This is all carried out electronically now. Other examples of innovation in the cockpit include the electronic flight bag we introduced in 2004, which uploads information to the pilot about each flight. Because it's electronic, it allows us to transmit far more information, which improves safety.

3.1

You can take that kind of communications capability much further. Today, the data link transmission speeds from the cockpit to the ground are relatively slow. But what if you had better compression techniques that allowed you to move real-time data, continuously, from the aircraft's engines to the ground? That would mean the operations center would know instantly if there was a problem. We are also talking with scientists who have developed new compression techniques that enable live video to be transmitted over very narrow bandwidth. Again, this technology all has to be commercialized—but it exists.

Sometimes it is just a question of timing. Seven years ago we designed a solution called Dominium, which tracks trucks using a low orbiting satellite. We were days away from signing our first freight carrier when a large round of tax increases was announced, including significant rises in fuel tax. The trucking companies were immediately hit, and suddenly none of them was in a position to buy our technology. So we put it on the shelf.

Since then, the business case for the technology has remained valid, of course. Every time a driver crosses a state line he has to fill in a number of forms. By using transducers and sensors around the truck, we can work out its mileage, fuel, and all the other items that need to be checked, which can be automatically transmitted to a truck company's operations center so that drivers no longer need to stop at state borders. With the current price of fuel, however, it is doubtful that trucking companies will be moving forward with new technology capital investments.

Sometimes, it is simply a question of thinking out of the box. We looked at a scanning system that examines a piece of luggage or a container and reads the atomic numbers of every material inside. If you think of all the ways you could use this kind of classification, it could be huge. Not only could you use it to examine containers, you could also sail a ship into a port through a huge arch that could detect anything in the whole ship. This is still very much at the experimental stage, however.

Migrating technology across industries

This kind of thinking reflects one of the most important benefits we can bring to the transportation industry, which is to help migrate technologies from one sector to another. The aviation industry is the most advanced in technical terms, and in many ways it acts as an incubator for rail and sea.

ARINC installed the command centers for train control at about 20 sites in the U.S. We applied the same technologies that we do for air traffic control, but on a two-dimensional basis. Transit authorities in states such as New York, New Jersey, and Washington have all put these systems in and they allow trains to operate more effectively, improving safety at the same time. New York and Jersey Transit have some of the most complex tunnel tracking systems in the world, but we helped them put in new technology that will allow them to move more trains, in a given time through a major complex, more safely.

If you go to a transit company and say, "I have the most advanced, gee-whiz technology" you may well scare them. But if you bring in technology that is already proven in other systems and has been around three or four years, they will accept it.

From a homeland defense point of view, many people have some skepticism about the effectiveness of airports' passenger security systems—although I believe they are fairly effective. But take a look at containers and marine ports. You can talk to heads of marine ports today and they will tell you that they do not even know where a significant percentage of containers in their ports are. Likewise, four or five years ago, ARINC was involved in surface transportation to track containers hauled by trucks—and even here we did not know where some of the containers were in the United States, because they are not tracked.

We are now working on a prototype tracking system that could bring about a revolution in how we manage containers. We also think that if we tie this kind of technology to some of our existing systems, we could deliver a total, secure system for ports. For example, ARINC developed Pilot Mate, a three-dimensional GPS tracking system that is used by pilots when they bring big ships into port. We also developed a marine information system for a seaport in Texas, where we tied together a number of different databases. And we provide perimeter security for most of the nuclear stations in the United

States. So we are trying to pick up all of the IT-type capabilities that we have used in the air and on the surface and deliver them as part of homeland security solutions for marine ports.

The aviation industry is the most advanced in technical terms and in many ways it acts as an incubator for rail and sea.

This is not just about migrating technology from one sector to another—it is also about replicating the kinds of standards that prevail in the aviation sector. Aircraft and airlines have to operate all around the world, so they need a degree of commonality between systems and in the way they move data. An aircraft flying from the United States to the U.K. has to be able to deal with any type of nav-com or surveillance system on the ground, and there has been a lot of standardization in the aviation community to ensure safety. It takes time to get consensus, but you have to get it or those aircraft will not be able to fly globally.

3.1

One of the problems in surface transportation is that those standards do not exist. We are involved with the Federal Highways Department on an initiative to develop a smart highway—but how can you communicate with different vehicles built by different manufacturers? With trains, the train control systems and communications infrastructure have to be standardized—if there is no standard, you cannot transfer and move data. So we are trying to take what we do in aviation and be a catalyst to help develop those standards across the U.S., agreeing upon a common approach that achieves higher levels of safety.

Change will come
I think we need to be realistic about the pace of change. When I consider what is likely to happen in terms of the U.S. air traffic control system over the next 10 years, I think in many respects it will be slightly advanced, but not much.

Similarly, there will be some level of technology applied to increase capacity at airports, but I do not think you will see a huge difference in the number of new runways, for example.

At the same time, however, there will be a number of significant developments where technology will play a key role. For example, military Unmanned Aerial Vehicles will have to fly in commercial airspace across the U.S., so we need to tie them into the same technology so that they comply with the flight plans for passenger aircraft.

In many respects the transportation industry has no choice but to embrace this change. I have an IP telephone, a BlackBerry, one telephone number worldwide—and I am in constant communication 24 hours a day. The airline industry will need to cater for my communications needs. We have already developed Ku-Band communications for the commercial jet community (we initially went to the commercial airlines with the same type of system to allow high-speed Internet links, but after 9/11 there was no capital available). We can already deliver a broadband network to business jets and, with a new antenna design we are building, we will have up to 10MB. That is as good as anything you have in your house, so we can effectively provide a full office in the sky. As we move forward, we will be able to use that same pipe to move operational data for the airlines about weather, flight planning, and so forth, which will make air travel even safer.

***

The big issues for the future will be to find ways to overcome the institutional hurdles that sometimes slow us down when implementing new technologies.

***

We have also announced pico-cell technology that allows you to use your cell phone on an aircraft via a satellite, and we have signed our first airline in Europe. It also handles data (voice and audio) to your BlackBerry. There are still some regulatory issues in Europe, but we went there first because they are ready to go. It is going to be two years in the U.S. before we get regulatory agreement.

All of these examples demonstrate that it is not hard to find solutions from a technology point of view—but technology alone is not the issue. Bear in mind that in 1975 we were developing the first aeronautical satellite for aviation communications over the oceans—institutional issues stopped its progress. The big issues for the future will be to find ways to overcome the institutional hurdles that sometimes slow us down when implementing new technologies, and to ensure that we can develop a compelling commercial proposition for each of them.

If we succeed in doing that, we will be better placed to tackle the many challenges that the transportation industry faces going forward.

About ARINC Inc.

ARINC was incorporated in 1929 as Aeronautical Radio, Inc. and was chartered by the Federal Radio Commission (FRC) to serve as the airline industry's "single licensee and coordinator of radio communication". Owned by the four major airlines of the day, it took on responsibility for ground-based aeronautical radio stations and for ensuring station compliance with FRC rules and regulations. Today, it is a US$800 million provider of transportation communications and systems engineering solutions.

3.1

Customer-driven innovation— the future of rail

André Navarri I Executive VP, Bombardier Inc. and President,
Bombardier Transportation, Canada

R ail was at the forefront of economic development in the industrial era, acting as the key mode of transportation in Europe and America. At the leading edge of transportation before roads, this was its golden age.

Relationship between US GDP growth and railroad development

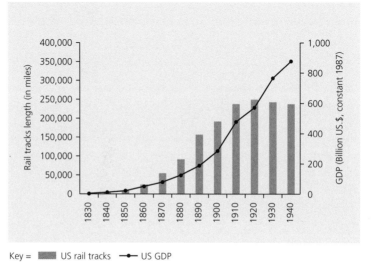

Key = US rail tracks — US GDP

Figure 1.
Sources: http://www.pbs.org/wgbh/
amex/streamliners/timeline/,
http://www.bts.dot.gov/publications/
national_transportation_statistics/
2004/html/table_01_01.html,
http://canback.com/usgdp.xls

In the US, rail travel tripled between 1896 and 1916, and trains carried 95 per cent of all inter-city transportation up to 1910. In the UK, birthplace of the industry, the railway companies, with the impetus of a new technology and a stock market bubble behind them, were building almost 7,000 miles of railway every decade between 1830 and 1930, with the peak occurring in the 1860s.

While some write off rail as a 19th-century technology, the facts tell a different story, one of modern technology and innovation. In particular, we see rail operators becoming ever more customer-centric, a theme to which I shall return.

From the mid-1960s to the early 1990s, the rail industry was characterised by the introduction of increasingly sophisticated propulsion and train control systems, followed by computer-based propulsion control. Over the past 10 to 15 years, electronic train control systems have been at the heart of new developments.

The prospects for the future are good, as decision-makers rediscover the advantages of rail, including its increased capacity compared to roads. Occupying one-third of the space that roads use, there is no congestion and the environment benefits, too. It also offers mobility to those who cannot benefit from the car—juniors, seniors, and the disadvantaged especially. For example, three in 10 homes in Britain do not own a car—some 13 million people. Even in homes with a car, it is not always available to everyone. For them, the rail network is a key mode of mobility.

3.2

All this means that there is now a greater and growing understanding that rail is a key transport mode for the future, especially in Europe where the infrastructure is already very well developed.

In Europe, there are 27 cities with a population of more than one million, and most could not survive if public transportation stopped working. Regional and inter-city rail networks are also extremely well positioned to become part of a homogeneous, continent-wide rail network.

As an example of rail's position as a popular and strong alternative to other modes of transportation, research shows that when fast train services start between two cities, they normally take 70 to 80 per cent of market share, compared to air travel.

> There is now a greater and growing understanding that rail is a key transport mode for the future.

That decision-makers now understand this is demonstrated by the European Commission's (EC) reaffirmation of its prioritisation of rail transportation. In Europe, the EC's, governments', and regions' biggest budget items fall into three main areas: healthcare, employment, and rail transportation.

Many of rail transportation's challenges result from both its historic nature and the long-lived nature of the infrastructure. Among the biggest challenges, especially in Europe, is that many countries' networks were built on a single-country rather than continent-wide basis.

Yet the European Union has decided to institute a fully interoperable rail system across Europe over the next 10 to 20 years. When finished, a train will be able to run from Rotterdam to Naples under a unified signalling system and without needing to switch between six or seven different electrical propulsion systems.

In terms of rail tracks, the only problems are Spain and Portugal, where a different track gauge prevails. When it comes to signalling systems, platforms, and the local regulations that govern the systems, these are all different. The real challenge now is to bring all these together into a single, Europe-wide railway.

So standardisation and interoperability are challenges. It means that, even when decision makers understand the benefits of rail, they need to make a bigger investment up-front compared to roads or other modes of transportation. When making that decision, they also need to understand and consider the total life cost of the system as well as the indirect benefits of rail transportation, such as reducing congestion and pollution.

However, persuading governments at all levels that large, up-front investments in rail infrastructure can show a return within their terms of office, is likely to remain a challenge, which will retard progress. One example is the funding of the UK end of the Channel Tunnel and the fast rail link into the capital. While the tunnel itself was outsourced entirely to the private sector, the link is a public-private partnership and is scheduled to be fully open by 2007, 13 years after opening of the tunnel in 1994.

Willingness to overcome standardisation and interoperability issues exists, with the benefit of standards defined by governmental bodies at local, national, and continent-wide level. Legislatures such as the EC already play a large part in shaping the rail industry and will continue to do so.

For example, the EC set up the Eurovignette system, where heavy goods vehicles will pay an annual charge related to the damage they cause to the environment and roads. The money is used to finance rail transportation, in order to reestablish parity between the two modes, taking into account issues such as pollution. This then allows a fair cost comparison to be made.

This use of public funds is an increasing trend. With access to workplaces becoming a higher priority, some cities use corporate taxes to pay for the transport infrastructures that employees need to get to and from their places of work. Clear benefits for both employer and employee ensue. In some places, such as Paris, a three-hour commute to and from work is commonplace, so enterprises understand that paying for the development of the transportation infrastructure is in their own interests.

In London the local authority has imposed a congestion charge in order to relieve the city centre of car traffic, which helps tilt the balance towards rail, as well as improving the local environment.

We are at a turning point, with rail gaining market share for both passengers and freight.

Looking further afield, the problem of managing growth and environmental issues is not confined to Europe. Chinese leaders have asked Bombardier for advice on how to meet the challenges of a growing economy. They know that if they do not soon decide to upgrade their transportation systems, they will face massive pollution and congestion problems. They also know that if government does nothing, in 10 years there will be five times as many trucks on the roads. These issues need to be addressed centrally by government, as privateers such as truck owners cannot be expected to make transportation planning, five to 10 years into the future, one of their priorities.

3.2

Persuading governments at all levels that large, up-front investments in rail infrastructure can show a return within their terms of office is likely to remain a challenge.

It is encouraging that politicians are clearly starting to look beyond the next election and seeing that making the right decisions for the longer term brings benefits not just for the public but also for them, politically. This is being shown in the way that leaders are operating in places such as London, Paris, Tokyo, and Bejing.

Rail has definite opportunities for the future, not least of which is increasing capacity by reducing headway—the distance between trains—using computers, signalling, and radio technologies. It is a direction denied to the road industry, as a road's capacity to carry trucks is both finite and reaching its limit. In some parts of Europe, you can see a continuous stream of trucks on the motorways, 24 hours a day.

I believe that modern IT brings many benefits to passengers but, of these, three are key: passenger communications, asset maintenance, and asset tracking. They all involve communications—between passengers and the Internet, and between the trains themselves and the operator.

Passenger communications

The first is in the area of communications. Most trains carry very little modern communications technology and, in some areas, even using a mobile phone is not possible. We believe this has to change, and some operators are moving in that direction. This will involve installing on-train Wi-Fi networking, along with GSM cabling to allow continuous mobile coverage, even in tunnels.

This gives customer-centric train operators a key advantage, as passengers are able to remain connected. You cannot compute and drive. Even on a 20-minute commute, there's no reason you should not be able to browse the Internet and access email. Experience shows that passengers will often wait until the next train if they know it is more modern and offers them a more comfortable journey. Since this kind of service makes passengers happy, it can be used to increase passenger numbers.

Asset maintenance

Second on the list is information. It is essential to efficiency that the train operator knows as much as possible about the trains, in particular train condition and state of maintenance. We need to evolve from the manual processes of ticking checkboxes with a ballpoint pen, waiting for parts to break, followed by the train going to the depot, being inspected, ordering spare parts, waiting for parts, and so on.

With today's pervasive networking and communications capabilities, remote software/firmware upgrades will become the norm and may, in fact, create positive incremental economic impact.

Increasingly today, we see onboard maintenance diagnostic systems that monitor the condition of the train and those critical components that suffer from wear and tear. They can then send information in advance about potential failures, allowing maintenance depots to ready themselves in advance for the work. For example, Bombardier's trains in use on France's regional rail network can send information in advance to the depot using GSM.

Systems are not yet perfect, however, and potential cost savings remain unrealised. One specific area is the monitoring of critical areas such as wheel bearings. Today's technology allows the measurement of heat and vibration on the axles, but most operators rely on frequent bearing replacement cycles. Yet, on dismantling the bogies, they often find that only about 20 per cent of bearings actually need replacing. With tomorrow's technology we will be able to ensure bearing replacement takes place only as and when required, resulting in significant savings.

Other benefits of technology on new trains include the ability to debug systems more quickly. All products as complex as trains will exhibit problems when new, but with predictive maintenance and fault reporting, we can eliminate these much more quickly than before.

Asset tracking

Asset tracking technology can also bring big savings. This allows operators to optimise fleet usage by combining knowledge about each train's condition with the ability to pinpoint its position at any point in time.

All these systems make a useful individual contribution. Maximum value can be extracted from integrating them, bringing together information about mobile assets, the fixed infrastructure, the signalling using pervasive networking, and standard communications protocols such as the Internet Protocol.

One other fairly major and probably intractable issue remains. The rail business is fairly conservative and products have a long lifespan; the typical life of a train car is around 30 years. The IT business, on the other hand, is accustomed to product lifecycles of under one-tenth of that. Following Moore's Law, where the amount of computing power doubles every 18 months or two years, people replace their mobile phones every year and their PCs every two to three years.

3.2

The industry needs to find a way to avoid the train operator facing almost instant obsolescence when installing industry-standard, off-the-shelf technology in a train car, followed by considerable ongoing costs for upgrades. They need to feel comfortable that key subsystems of a two-year-old train will not need replacement because the technology it contains is out of date. We believe that with today's pervasive networking and communications capabilities, remote software/firmware upgrades will become the norm and may, in fact, create positive incremental economic impact.

We are not turning away from these problems, though we do not always have a complete answer. But we are keenly aware that this issue needs to be addressed.

As in any mode of public transportation, safety is a big issue, and one where technology has a role to play. Speed can be controlled and signalling can be improved, for instance. France's high-speed trains have a very impressive safety record, with no injuries at all. But, whether in aviation or rail, most incidents happen as a result of human error. It is possible to eliminate human error to some extent by removing people from system management and increasing our reliance on computers. On the other hand, if someone is determined to commit suicide on the railway, for example, there is often little you can do. That said, rail is, and we intend to ensure that it remains, the safest mode of transportation.

Bombardier's philosophy, always to innovate, is core to that effort. In rail as in aerospace, we will always go to market with the most innovative products that we believe are appropriate.

In developing innovative products, we undergo a very formalised review process that consumes large amounts of management time. As the lead time between concept and reality can be five years, it involves projecting forward to product release time, taking into consideration issues such as future costs, technology and market changes, competition and global economic issues. If we want to continue leading the industry, we now have to produce the most innovative products for our customers.

> Even though the rail operating industry is inherently conservative, when you examine operators' experiments—for example, with Wi-Fi—innovation is starting to produce the right results, with increasing passenger numbers.

The rail manufacturing industry will evolve to become a maximum of three, maybe two main players. Our customers, once nearly all state-owned, will increasingly become a mix of state and privately owned, with more joint private/public ventures. However, the method of funding does not make a huge difference to operators' attitudes about innovation. Contrary to expectations, some publicly owned operators are very innovative, while private companies can be conservative. In fact, major innovations often come via the public sector because they are the only ones with the freedom to take risks.

The big trend is for operators of all kinds to become increasingly customer-centric and, for us, this is good news. For example, Deutsche Bahn now asks itself who its customers are, and is aware that passengers and freight shippers have alternatives. Very few railways now believe their job is simply to fulfil a government mandate to carry passengers. This is disappearing—very few of them remain. Whether you look at SNCF, Deutsche Bahn, or NS, their focus is on how to compete against aeroplanes, roads, and other modes of transportation.

This is why we are optimistic that, even though the rail operating industry is inherently conservative, when you examine operators' experiments—for example, with Wi-Fi—innovation is starting to produce the right results, with increasing passenger numbers.

This stems from a greater focus on the customers' needs and wants. It means providing them with up-to-date information, with technology that allows them to continue working, or to be entertained. Keeping them happy and keeping them as passengers are the key drivers.

Continuing along that track, further innovation could lead to trains that are driverless, faster, more efficient, and that run with reduced headway. Existing systems have been known to run headways of between 60 and 120 seconds. Freight will be more efficient as customers will be able to ship goods from point to point without having to deal with frontiers. A reliable, dependable, and cost-effective service means the operators and their customers benefit, costs are reduced, and a virtuous circle is created.

Passengers will benefit from easier inter-modal journeys. With the growth of communications, passengers will be able to plan and order their journeys using whatever mode of transportation is appropriate. They will travel in an environment where they can feel at home, and have access to video, Wi-Fi, and other mobile communications.

It is clear that passengers will benefit as rail transport becomes more important with increasing mobility. If you doubt this, look at the amount of travelling that students do today. Previously, they might stay in one place much of the time, but now they move around quite regularly. If we can show them today that rail is an exciting, reliable method of transport, they will be tomorrow's customers.

3.2

Transportation will become an extension of the home or office, allowing passengers to do whatever they want, whether listening to music, watching TV, or working, all without the kinds of interruptions and distractions involved in road travel.

Rail will be the easiest way of going from point to point in an enjoyable, relaxed atmosphere, with the benefit of progressive technology—the big enabler.

Rail faces an exciting and challenging future. The way operators approach the market is changing, while their customers, freight companies, and passengers continue to increase their expectations of rail.

About Bombardier

Bombardier is a US$17 billion company with two main activities: aerospace and rail. Aerospace brings in some US$10 billion in revenues while Bombardier Transportation serves the rail industry and earns the remaining US$7 billion.

Serving a diversified customer base around the world, Bombardier Transportation is the global leader in the rail equipment manufacturing and servicing industry. Its wide range of products includes passenger rail vehicles and total transit systems. It also manufactures locomotives, freight cars, bogies, propulsion, and controls, and provides rail control solutions.

Driving structural change in aviation maintenance

August Wilhelm Henningsen I CEO and Chairman of the Executive Board, Lufthansa Technik, Germany

Airline maintenance has undergone fundamental change in recent years, thanks to the cumulative effect of information technologies and business process change. Thirty or 40 years ago, airlines used to focus predominantly on safety and reliability; today, while safety remains the top priority, aircraft and their supporting systems have been so finely tuned that certain aspects of reliability can be taken for granted. Now, with the industry under constant pressure to reduce costs, attention is turning to new priorities, with many airlines reexamining the way they manage their maintenance operations.

In the past, major airlines used to control every aspect of their business, from processing and transporting passengers to managing the technical work on the aircraft. Now, both the long-established players and the newer breed of low-cost airlines are increasingly looking to outsource this work to third-party Maintenance, Repair, and Overhaul (MRO) specialists. This brings enormous efficiencies to the industry, but it is also changing the competitive landscape. Today the MRO industry is growing by 4 to 6 per cent per annum.

Maintenance, Repair, and Overhaul Market

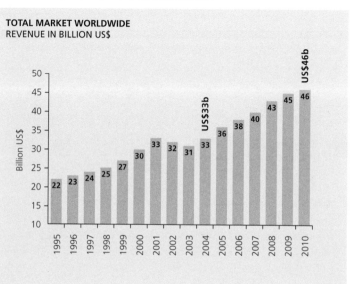

TOTAL MARKET WORLDWIDE REVENUE IN BILLION US$

Figure 1. Data includes all commercial jet types, excluding business jets. Modifications (estimate US$3B), no price escalation in constant US$. Sources: Lufthansa Technik, 2003–010 MRO Initiative 2005, 1995–2002. Calculated with average per aircraft.

Just as the airlines are adapting their business models, so the MRO industry is going through its own evolutionary change. Part of that change is structural, part is about the way it leverages technology, from the wireless networks that keep passengers connected in the air, to asset management and documentation systems that give us control over the lifecycle of aircraft components. Making these changes is not always easy, but it is the only way to build a platform to provide high-quality, cost-effective service.

> When you have 500 passengers on board, you cannot keep them waiting while you decide how to tackle a maintenance issue.

3.3

Reliability: key to change in aviation

Keeping aeroplanes well maintained is a huge challenge. For one thing, they are worked intensively, usually enduring up to 15 hours' flight time every day. For another, there are enormous commercial pressures on the maintenance industry to perform. Airlines simply cannot afford to have expensive aircraft sitting on the tarmac any longer than they have to—and when you have 500 passengers on board, you cannot keep them waiting while you decide how to tackle a maintenance issue. As a result, our industry's priorities are to drive down the amount of maintenance required to keep these aircraft safely in the air and to resolve any problems that might arise as quickly as possible.

When 707s were first introduced in the 1960s, airlines were responsible for every aspect of operating and maintaining them. It was no easy task. Information was hard to come by because there was such a low volume of aeroplanes in circulation, and there was no easy way to share information by fax or email. So once an airline took responsibility for an aircraft, it was pretty much on its own. As a result, airlines had to develop their own competencies internally and, inevitably, the two areas on which they focused most intensely were safety and reliability. Because aircraft performance was relatively poor 40 years ago, reliability actually became a competitive differentiator.

Over the last four decades, the aircraft, engine and component manufacturers, airlines, and MRO providers have worked hand-in-hand to improve quality, reliability, and safety. In our maintenance and overhaul divisions at Lufthansa Technik, for example, we have representatives from all major manufacturers such as Boeing, Airbus, GE, Honeywell and Thales. If we encounter a problem, we discuss it openly: we put forward proposals on how it can be fixed and then the manufacturers research it and come back with a solution. We are the technical arm of Lufthansa German Airlines. All the knowledge accumulated over the years has been pooled to help the ongoing maintenance of today's aircraft.

We continue to learn about the aeroplanes as existing models age and new developments are introduced. By understanding the way that system behaviour changes during an aircraft's lifetime, over time we can eliminate work in some areas and switch our focus to more problematic areas—some structural problems that we could not have envisaged five years ago, for example, may be a big problem today. So we are constantly shifting our focus on each individual aeroplane, and constantly learning. We always say that the aircraft manufacturers know the strengths of the aeroplane—but we know the weaknesses!

We are also using our knowledge to influence future aircraft designs, specifying systems in a way that eliminates faults we have encountered in the past in order to reduce the ongoing maintenance cost. Since the beginning of the 1980s, for example, we have been working with the manufacturers and airlines to test carbon fibre structures for secondary structures at fuselages and primary structures such as at the empennage. Ultimately, if the behaviour of the material is suitable, we may well see complete aircraft built out of carbon fibre, which could cost dramatically less to maintain and even to build.

> While improved reliability has helped the major airlines reduce maintenance per flight hour, it has also added to the competitive pressures they face by adding the low-cost carrier model to the industry.

As a result of all of these efforts, the amount of maintenance per flight hour continues to decline. Components today are three to four times more reliable than they were 15 to 20 years ago, and new ideas are constantly being investigated to improve our aircraft monitoring systems and processes.

1. BusinessWeek 20 June 2005.

To illustrate this, a recent report[1] estimates that the benefits of the Boeing 787's skin being composed entirely from carbon fibre and similar composite materials will include: 20 per cent fuel savings; cost savings through faster and cheaper assembly; improved passenger comfort as cabins can withstand higher pressurisation for a closer-to-normal atmosphere; and an average increase in 'corrosion and crack' inspection intervals.

New business models

As the reliability of aircraft has improved, the focus within the industry has shifted. Safety remains our top priority, of course; our maintenance procedures are very detailed, and after they are agreed internally, they are also approved by the manufacturers and the authorities. But with reliability now almost a given, there is additional emphasis on reducing cost. This is driving fundamental change across the industry. For the airlines, it means selecting the most cost-effective means of carrying out maintenance, including utilising best practice business models from other industries, such as outsourcing. For the MRO sector, it means finding ways to reduce the cost of delivering those services.

Outsourcing—different potentials within the industry

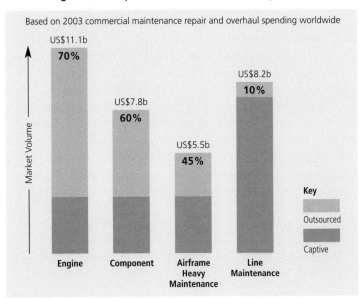

3.3

Figure 2.
Source: Aerostrategy 2003,
Lufthansa Tecknik's Surveys MRO
Network Forecast, Data 2004.

Ten years ago, outsourcing was barely on the airline industry's radar: each airline kept all of the technical expertise it needed in-house. But September 11th created a crisis within the industry that exacerbated underlying problems such as high costs and complex business processes; problems that have been fuelled by the emergence of low-cost airlines.

Ironically, while improved reliability has helped the major airlines reduce maintenance per flight hour, it has also added to the competitive pressures they face by adding the low-cost carrier model to the industry. Forty years ago, I would have needed an extensive technical infrastructure in place before I could consider setting up an airline. Today, I can lease my aircraft, hire pilots, employ an MRO services company and within six months, be ready to go. If you have the financing in place, it really is that easy; the cost of entry for new competitors has been dramatically lowered.

We are seeing evidence of this within our own customer base. Our strongest market is Europe, but we are also expanding in Asia, in the Middle East and in North America. We recently signed a contract with Spirit Airlines in North America, for example, to help it transition to next-generation aeroplanes; we will be supporting the aircraft in terms of materials, logistics and engineering. In India, where a number of low-cost carriers are opening up, we have signed an agreement with a new airline called Kingfisher, and we also serve Jet Airways.

In the past, an airline would have needed around two years to build that kind of capability; now it's becoming a matter of weeks. We are able to help by providing what we call an 'à la carte' service, where we 'cut and paste' different components of our portfolio to meet our clients' specific needs. We take a little bit of engineering skill for the A340, add in the relevant materials, provide some trouble-shooters, connect the software and we're away. What sounds so easy is backed by experienced engineers and support functions like material provision and logistics. Following this concept, all maintenance stations of our customers are closely linked to Lufthansa Technik's hubs in Frankfurt and Hamburg to assure the highest performance and reliability.

This is a new business model that divides up responsibility within the airline sector: the airline takes care of the flying and the passengers, and organisations like ours manage the technical aspects. This model presents great opportunities for airlines starting from scratch that have no technical legacy; but for the major airlines, it can be more difficult. Many of them already have a large technical organisation, along with assets such as hangars, buildings and of course people, so it is much harder for them to take the decision to outsource. For one thing, it is never easy to compare the cost of retaining technical services in-house versus outsourcing: very few companies in any industry are able to isolate all of the processes related to one business activity and cost them, so it is hard for them to establish an accurate, comparative business case.

A number of companies in the United States have already gone down this route. Most of the major airlines used to have a big technical organisation, but it is now outsourced. While some carriers are starting the process of sourcing more and more different services externally, others already outsource complete packages like heavy maintenance or engine overhaul.

It is important to stress that we are not immune to these seismic industry changes at Lufthansa Technik. Around 50 per cent of our business is with Lufthansa itself, which is also in competition with other airlines. This means we have to make sure that our products are more than competitive in comparison to the world market. We have had to be particularly creative in Germany, where costs for manpower-intensive work are high.

That is why we have effectively outsourced our own heavy maintenance and structural checks for aeroplanes, by buying companies with a better cost platform and then managing them, either as wholly owned subsidiaries or as joint ventures with other partners.

We have also developed centres of excellence to deliver our services. With Philippines Airlines, whose aircraft we maintain, we set up a joint venture that adds our engineering expertise and management skills to create a very cost-effective centre of excellence for A330 and A340 heavy maintenance operations.

While some carriers are starting the process of sourcing more and more different services externally, others already outsource complete packages like heavy maintenance or engine overhaul.

Lufthansa Technik has also carried out something similar in Europe and has facilities in Shannon, Ireland and Budapest, Hungary, where we run checks on narrow-bodied aeroplanes. Likewise, we have established our specialist engine and component business in Hamburg, Germany. All of this allows us to reduce the cost of delivering high-quality services.

3.3

Technology challenges and opportunities

These efficiencies have been complemented by a number of developments in the information technology field. Historically, some of the most significant advances have been in the cockpit, hooking up navigation and flight systems to improve reliability and make life easier for the pilots. Over the last 20 years we have also seen enormous progress in monitoring systems. We can now monitor the condition of an engine, send the data by satellite or VHF to the ground and compare it with the characteristics of a perfectly-performing engine. Where preset performance parameters are breached, an engineer will get a message requesting analysis, and he or she can delve back into the engine's history to check on its age, maintenance history, trends and so forth. Similarly, we can check things like pressurisation systems and hydraulics— sending messages to the cockpit and to the maintenance organisation.

Going forward, it will be in the cabin and management systems where we will see some of the most interesting developments. Lufthansa Technik already provides a system called 'NICE' (Network Integrated Cabin Equipment), which replaces the separate networks that control entertainment and cabin functions with a single system that manages all these functions over one network.

We have a great deal of expertise in this area: our VIP division equips business, government and other VIP jets with high-speed data links via satellite that can receive live TV programmes, and we have developed a system that uses cabin panels as sound diaphragms to eliminate the need for conventional loudspeakers.

Likewise, we are implementing wireless networks in cabins of passenger aircraft and undertake the regulatory approval. We have talked for years about connecting passengers to their offices so that they can work effectively in the air using email and the Internet. The use of a wireless system is very efficient for the passenger but also for simplification of the installation, since we do not need to hook up every seat with wires. We may even see wireless audio systems for entertainment systems, which will also bring costs down and give greater flexibility.

> We can now monitor the condition of an engine, send the data by satellite or VHF to the ground and compare it with the characteristics of a perfectly performing engine.

As far as our own management systems go, we have installed SAP's enterprise software system across the company to handle everything from the repair process, warehousing and supply chain, through the accounting and billing processes, to our customer management systems. This is essential to the way we operate.

We have more than US$1 billion in assets that we use to supply our customers' aeroplanes, and we need to make sure that their use is optimised. If a computer or a hydraulic machine is failing, then we need to be able to replace it with the same kind of unit, bring the faulty component back, repair it and make it available for the next loop. Our system gives us insight into this whole process, including the documentation of the aircraft components and engines. Each aircraft component is serialised, and we need to have records all the way back to its initial manufacture, logging details of the aircraft in which it flew, who repaired it and when. This is a huge undertaking that requires us to monitor parts that travel around the world, and we have undertaken much work to streamline these processes.

Radio Frequency Identification (RFID) is also emerging as a key technology in our industry. While people commonly think of it in the context of tracking passenger luggage, it will also play an important role in monitoring components as they move through repair shops and warehouses and into and out of aeroplanes. This is an extension of a project we started 10 years ago to apply bar coding to as many of our components as possible—we have even developed bar codes with heat resistance of up to 500°F or 600°F to use in hot pneumatic and hydraulic components.

Deploying this kind of system means we no longer have to write down serial numbers, which is prone to human error and causes major headaches when we need to check irregularities. The last thing we want is to have assets worth hundreds of thousands of dollars sitting idle while we try to clarify a handwritten remark.

Looking ahead

The speed with which these new technologies are adopted will be driven by a combination of demand and the realities of the business case. Email access, for example, may become a competitive differentiator: if there is a choice of two airlines travelling the same route at the same price, business travellers will select the one that keeps them connected. Lufthansa has 50 per cent of its aircraft wired up now, and we are speeding up the installation process as fast as we can so that we can eventually guarantee the facility on all of our long-range aeroplanes. At some point passengers will demand it—once a third or more of the world's aircraft are equipped, it will shift from being a pleasant surprise to something that passengers expect as standard. But it does take time to get all of the aeroplanes into the hangar to equip them.

3.3

There are major changes sweeping the airline business, but, as I have stated, our industry's priorities are to drive down the amount of maintenance required to keep aircraft safely in the air and to address any problems as soon as possible. Technology is going to continue to play a significant role in this. Only with the ongoing developments in technology are we going to be able to achieve even greater reliability and safety standards with increased visibility of information and increased integration of all aspects of the business.

About Lufthansa Technik

Deutsche Lufthansa AG is a world leading airline company. As an aviation group, Lufthansa focuses on the core competencies of its six business areas: passenger traffic; logistics; Maintenance, Repair and Overhaul (MRO); catering; leisure travel and IT services. In 2004 the Group achieved revenues of €17 billion.

Lufthansa Technik is the world market leader in the MRO of commercial aircraft, their engines and components. With customised programmes for maintenance and state-of-the-art repair procedures, Lufthansa Technik continuously assures the reliability and availability of its customers' fleets. The five business units of Lufthansa Technik (Maintenance, Airframe Overhaul, Component Services, Engine Services and VIP Services) serve more than 540 customers worldwide.

Authorities

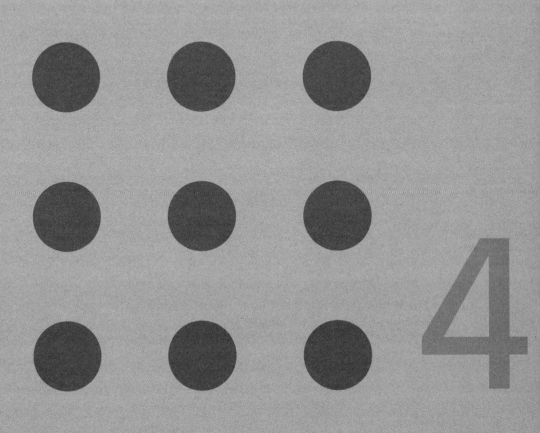

Challenges for European transport policy in 2010

François Lamoureux | Director-General, Transportation and Energy Directorate, European Commission, Belgium

At the beginning of the 21st century, transport is very much at the heart of our socio-economic system and remains the fundamental driver for industry and our way of life. The transport sector in the European Union (EU) accounts for expenditure of some €1,000 billion, generates over 10 per cent of the Union's GDP and employs more than 10 million people. It facilitates commercial, economic and cultural exchange, helping to bring Europe's citizens closer together, and so contributing to European integration. It is therefore the focus for the EU's most important common policies.

The European Union transport policy, which has been highly successful, is to sacrifice neither economic growth in an enlarged Europe nor freedom of movement—especially since people in our society increasingly view mobility as a freedom and a basic right. So we try to take into account a number of aspects when developing policy and balance the social, economic, political and technological issues.

Naturally, economic competitiveness has driven most reforms in recent years, but we have also seen strong interest in safety issues after disasters such as the sinking of the oil tankers Erika and Prestige, or the tragic accidents in road tunnels like the Mont-Blanc, St Gothard and, more recently, the Fréjus. The way forward is to make mobility systems more balanced, smarter and take into account growing environmental demands and the challenges of globalisation.

The policy core is contained in the European Commission's (EC) White Paper on European Transport Policy, launched in 2001. It proposed various solutions to maintain competitiveness while developing a sustainable transport model. Priority was given to three main axes: changing the modal split with a shift away from roads by 2010; eliminating bottlenecks and tackling congestion, and placing safety and quality at the heart of transport policy.

Analysis of today's European transport sector in general terms reveals mixed performance. While market integration has undoubtedly made progress over the last 10 or so years, with positive effects on the mobility of goods and people, it has not been accomplished equally.

Air transport is clearly one of Europe's integration success stories, with full liberalisation having been achieved. We are moving towards a new trans-Atlantic area, uniting the United States and the EU in a single aviation market, tackling issues such as traffic rights, ownership, safety and security

and competition disputes. There have also been some very positive improvements in maritime transport, although effort in this direction needs to be maintained. We still have work to do to improve safety further in this sector.

However, rail remains the lame duck of the various modes, especially in its role as transport for freight. Key among the reasons for this are the differences between the various national systems—technical and administrative—that account for significant delays at border crossings and therefore extra costs. These include different gauge widths, different systems for the supply of electrical current, differences in maximum axle loads for wagons and locomotives, and major differences in the organisation of rail traffic management systems. In terms of challenges for the future, rail transportation issues, in particular for freight, are the biggest.

4.1

> The European Union transport policy, which has been highly successful, is to sacrifice neither economic growth in an enlarged Europe nor freedom of movement.

So, as we move towards 2010, the EU Common Transport policy will have to face three main challenges: infrastructure, sustainability and the best uses for new technology.

European transport infrastructure

With a view to addressing the challenges ahead, we have concentrated our efforts on rail and maritime transport to improve their competitiveness and share of traffic. We are hopeful that by 2010, lorry queues in sensitive regions like the Alps and the Pyrénées will have disappeared, and between a third and half of freight will be transported by high-speed trains. Further, Europe will be fully connected from north to south and west to east, including the neighbouring countries, thanks to the realisation of the main axes and their interconnection.

This priority has resulted in new legislation, with priority being given to the development over the next 20 years of a key infrastructure initiative, the Trans-European Network for Transport (TEN-T). This is a major advance in economic competitiveness and a balanced and sustainable development of the EU that requires the interconnection and interoperability of national networks.

The objective we set with the White Paper in 2001 was to restore modal shares to their 1998 levels, with the longer-term aim of shifting the balance away from road by 2010. Specifically, we are looking for slower growth in road haulage (38 per cent instead of 50 per cent) and for the growth of rail and inland waterway transport to triple. This would result in a reduction of some 200 million tonnes in emissions of CO_2 to the atmosphere, the equivalent of around one quarter of all transport emissions in 1998. This is without doubt the biggest challenge.

Technological innovation provides an excellent opportunity for modal integration and performance optimisation, as well as safety improvements.

Funding is a key lever for achieving policy aims. We are currently addressing a number of different possibilities, from increases in funding through taxation to direct infrastructure charging. Whatever the eventual solution, it must reflect the real costs of each mode of transport with the aim of generating revenues to invest in new infrastructure.

Sustainable transport

Damage to the environment and congestion remain our major concerns. Today's modal split, heavily slanted towards road transport, is a major factor in both.

European transport systems are afflicted by chronic congestion. In addition to the environmental costs, calculations indicate that the financial burden of congestion costs one per cent of our GDP—about the same as it costs to run the European Union.

With 10 per cent of the road network now regularly congested, road transport bears a particularly heavy environmental responsibility, since it currently accounts for 44 per cent of freight traffic and 79 per cent of passenger transport but generates 84 per cent of the CO_2 emissions attributable to the transport sector. Meanwhile, airports are permanently congested as we all know, while 20 per cent of the European rail network is considered a bottleneck. Yet rail transport is in decline, with a market share of barely 8 per cent of freight and 6 per cent of passenger transport.

There are two reasons for the growth of road transport. First is the spectacular rise in car ownership, a symbol of freedom for every European of driving age. The accession of new member states is fuelling this trend—the level of car use in the new member states is catching up with Western Europe. Second is, the emergence of an economy in which just-in-time is the order of the day, and stocks have been shifted onto the roads. This trend will be reinforced as the new member states become progressively integrated into the internal market, leading to an explosion in traffic flows.

The current situation is not sustainable. Demand for mobility will not diminish, regardless of the state of the economy, so we have to treat it as a key constant. Yet without action to distribute the predicted increase more evenly between the different transportation modes, those emissions are likely to increase by 50 per cent between 1990 and 2010, and traffic could increase by 50 per cent by 2010 compared with its 1998 level. Moreover, the candidate countries, where rail traffic has a much higher market share than in the Community, have also witnessed a shift towards roads since the 1990s.

There is nothing inevitable about this, however; in the United States, the railways have a freight market share of 40 per cent, and in Japan they carry 30 per cent of passengers. However, it will not be easy for rail to relieve roads of their burden. The EU has adopted various packages of measures with detailed provisions on opening up markets for rail freight transport; the interoperability of high-speed and conventional rail systems; the conditions under which state aid can be granted and public service obligations and contracts can be concluded; and on access to rail networks. This piece of legislation is now coming into force and its benefits will start appearing soon .

4.1

It is possible to shift the balance but we need to take action quickly to reconcile the demand for transport with sustainable development. Technology is the key.

New technologies

Technological innovation provides an excellent opportunity for modal integration and performance optimisation, as well as for safety improvements and helping to make transport development environmentally sustainable.

The EU is very actively involved in technological innovation in transport. Its research and development programmes are promoting innovation upstream, while the trans-European networks lend themselves well to large-scale application.

IT can make an outstanding contribution here and the wide variety of applications now available represents a real opportunity to move towards a better future. Based on information and communications technologies, real Intelligent Transport Systems (ITS) products and services are already hard at work.

ITS have a wide range of applications including travel information and planning, traffic management, improving transportation for elderly and handicapped, freight and fleet management, electronic fee collection, transport safety, emergency and incident handling and life in the urban environment.

In the wake of research and technology development programmes, Community guidelines for the development of the TEN-T resulted in a number of Community measures and actions aimed at promoting the use of IT in transport. The TEN-T guidelines cover, among other things, telematics infrastructures for traffic management systems and traffic information services. Based on a broad vision of ITS deployment throughout Europe, the TEN-T will establish interconnections, interoperability and continuity between services on long-distance routes, in metropolitan areas and across borders.

It is a good example of how the EC and the private sector work together. The transportation industry knows that technological developments are essential to competitiveness and survival, and often takes the lead in their development. Meanwhile, the Commission tries to maximise harmonisation of and interoperability between different technologies at both European and international levels.

Many ITS projects also need a strong public sector commitment to kick-start them—promise of funding often provides the right attraction for private partners and helps convince the industry. This was the case with GALILEO for instance, which is now very attractive after an initial development boosted by the European Commission and the European Space Agency. The European system for radio-navigation by satellite, it is certainly the EU's biggest success in recent years.

GALILEO is also probably the most substantial European joint project since the adoption of the Euro. Its commercial and practical impact will go well beyond Europe's previous best efforts such as Arianne or Airbus, creating some 150,000 jobs in the EU and revenues of more than €10 billion. GALILEO will be operational in 2008 and, with 95 per cent of all urban areas covered at all times without interruption, it will provide a higher degree of precision, better reliability and more homogeneous coverage than GPS, which is dependent on the US military's goodwill.

Other examples of EU proposals based on ITS technologies include ambitious industrial projects like SESAME for Air Traffic Control and ERTMS (European Rail Traffic Management System) for railway systems interoperability. ERTMS is the new signalling and management system for Europe, the basis for rail interoperability throughout Europe.

The SESAME programme is Europe's air traffic control infrastructure modernisation initiative. It was originally launched by the equipment manufacturers but now receives the support and commitment of the whole air transport community. From that point of view, it is a world first. It combines technological, economic and regulatory aspects and will use the Single Sky legislation. As well as ensuring that aircraft equipment is consistent with ground-based technological developments, it is aimed at synchronising the implementation of new equipment Europe-wide.

If the EC's policies succeed, we will be looking at a Europe in the future that is very different from the one with which we are familiar today.

The transport policy must be in the best interests of Europe, its citizens and the environment as a whole. It will continue to drive transportation policy in the direction of sustainable development for all modes.

Technology is key to optimising usage of existing infrastructure capacity, and to harmonising systems across the EU.

The public sector has a key role to play in transportation, in terms of regulation and taking initiatives when needed, both replacing and working alongside the private sector as appropriate. This means providing the impetus, creating initiatives and taking balanced decisions to build a framework for more and better private commitment. This is particularly true for infrastructure build-outs, mainly because much investment is unlikely ever to be profitable. Such investments are as much about quality of life—on which you cannot put a price—as they are about economics.

4.1

The key is the aggressive use of new technologies that allow greater traffic management in an environment of growing demand for mobility. Technology is key to optimising usage of existing infrastructure capacity, and to harmonising systems across the EU, thereby increasing traffic flows and eliminating unnecessary delays and costs.

So the EC can and will continue enabling transportation systems that help provide a better environment for citizens and commerce alike by making Europe more connected, both internally and externally.

About the Directorate-General for Energy and Transport
The Directorate-General for Energy and Transport is responsible for developing and implementing European policies in the energy and transport field. Its mission is to ensure that energy and transport policies are designed for the benefit of all sectors of society: businesses, cities, rural areas and, above all, citizens. The energy and transport sectors are pivotal to the European way of life and to the functioning of the economy; as such their operation has to be responsible in economic, environmental, safety and social terms.

The Directorate-General for Energy and Transport carries out these tasks using legislative proposals and programme management, including the financing of projects.

Transportation policy trends in the United States:

Meeting the challenge of globalization and bringing the private sector into needed transportation infrastructure solutions

Jeffrey N. Shane I Under Secretary for Policy, Department of Transportation, U.S.

The future I want to discuss is one in which the private sector would play a much more prominent role in the construction, finance, and management of our nation's transportation infrastructure.

The deregulation of trucking, freight rail, and airlines has produced enormous welfare benefits for U.S. consumers. Vigorous competition in these industries has lowered prices and increased innovation. While each mode faces important long-run challenges, they remain unmatched in efficiency and productivity—particularly when compared to their more regulated international counterparts.

Unfortunately, we have not seen the same levels of innovation in the provision of the underlying infrastructure on which vital transportation services ultimately depend. In other words, we shouldn't simply conclude that our job is done because we took some bold steps a quarter of a century ago. The fact is that our job is far from done. Now, more than ever, we need to reevaluate the case for public infrastructure monopolies. Certainly, when compared to other deregulated network services such as telecommunications, the arguments for 100 percent public control of transportation infrastructure seem increasingly weak.

The current state of the transportation sector must also be considered against a backdrop of surging demand for transportation services across all modes and a global economy in which businesses are ever more reliant on logistics to meet their cost-reduction targets. Global trade now accounts for nearly a third of our nation's GDP, with goods coming in from Asia at a particularly breathtaking pace. The fact is that transportation is embedded in the global economy in a new, fundamental, and irreversible way. Transportation isn't merely a service to manufacturers; it is an essential part of the manufacturing process. It isn't merely a service to retailing; it is the way retailers maintain inventory. That's why congestion, if left unaddressed, will have far more serious economic consequences in the future than ever before in our history.

So why, one might ask, hasn't there been more private sector involvement in transportation infrastructure in the United States? Let me offer two big reasons. First, not many investors have the fortitude or, indeed, the audacity to compete with our huge public sector programs for financing transportation infrastructure. Second, and even more daunting, a great

many legal roadblocks effectively discourage private sector investment in our transportation infrastructure. The current ban on the use of pricing to reduce congestion on our nation's interstate highways is a perfect example of the kind of problem we face.

The fact is that transportation is embedded in the global economy in a new, fundamental, and irreversible way.

4.2

In a very recent report focusing on *21st Century Challenges*, the Government Accountability Office (GAO) noted that—

> The use of tolls, congestion pricing, and user fees holds promise for helping to solve congestion and mobility problems and provides new revenues for infrastructure improvements. However, the availability of competing federal grant funds and federal restrictions on tolling, pricing, and fees can work at cross purposes by dissuading state and local governments and transportation service providers from adopting these tools.

I certainly agree with that assessment. Clearly, there is much more we can do to unleash the energy of the market across all modes of transportation and to encourage private sector investment in transportation infrastructure. In fact, as GAO suggests in its report, we need to reexamine the role of government and the role of the private sector in the provision of transportation infrastructure to determine whether our current, government-centric model is as relevant to this century as it was to the last. As you can probably guess by now, I think the answer is no.

A historical perspective: limiting private sector investment

Over the last 30 years, a broad consensus gradually developed on the major features of federal transportation policy. While there were occasional differences along the way, both political parties have basically agreed on economic deregulation in the airline, trucking, and rail industries, and on federal government's role in transportation infrastructure financing. The basic premise has been to eliminate federal operating subsidies for transportation and to focus government efforts on infrastructure. The upshot of this approach has been that federal, state, and local governments—and not the private sector—have shouldered primary responsibility for the financing of transportation infrastructure.

Governments have been actively searching for new ways to fund infrastructure expansion in an effort to meet rising demand without having to raise taxes.

Another report issued by the GAO last year looked at private sector sponsorship of some major highway and transit projects in some detail. They found that private sector investment has been used only to a limited extent, and that, again, the private sector faces many challenges to becoming more actively involved in highway and transit projects because of limited opportunities and barriers to financial success. In particular, their research showed that:

- Only 23 states permitted private sector involvement in transportation projects, and only 20 of those states permitted private sector involvement in highway projects.
- Where state and local governments have solicited such participation, it occurred on mostly lower priority projects, such as toll roads built in anticipation of future growth.
- State and local governments traditionally build and finance highway and transit projects through their capital improvement programs using federal grant funds that reimburse about 80 percent of the costs.

Recent developments

There are some signs out there, however, that we may be moving towards an important inflection point in transportation policy. If these indications are in fact a harbinger of things to come, we may be closing in on a new consensus that would call for a substantially increased role for private sector financing of transportation infrastructure.

It is not hard to understand the motivation—a combination of increasing congestion and uncertainty about the sustainability of traditional sources of funding. As a result, state and local governments have been actively searching for new ways to fund infrastructure expansion in an effort to meet rising demand without having to raise taxes. There aren't very many examples, but the ones we have seen have enjoyed real success. These projects follow a model used widely in other countries whereby the government awards a concession to a private sector firm to build or improve a highway, bridge, or transit or railway line. The private sector firm pays the government for the concession and gets to keep the revenues.

Among the few examples thus far are:

The Trans Texas Corridor. In December 2004, the State of Texas announced a deal with Cintra, an international group of engineering, financial, and consulting firms headquartered in Madrid, to develop the Trans Texas Corridor. Cintra will invest US$6 billion to build a toll road between Dallas and San Antonio by 2010, and has agreed to pay the State US$1.2 billion for the concession. In return for building the new transportation corridor, Cintra proposes to negotiate a 50-year contract to maintain and operate the new highway as a toll road.

The Chicago Skyway. In January 2005, the City of Chicago announced that it had leased the 7.8-mile Chicago Skyway Toll Bridge System to a Cintra-Macquarie consortium for 99 years. Cintra-Macquarie paid the City of Chicago US$1.83 billion for the concession. Cintra-Macquarie will operate the facility and keep the toll revenues. The Chicago Skyway deal has aroused interest in other parts of the country, leading states like New York, Indiana, and New Jersey to look more closely at the possible privatization of their toll roads.

4.2

Go California. Also in 2005, the Schwarzenegger administration announced its "Go California" proposal, which would allow private firms to build new toll roads and High Occupancy Toll (HOT) lanes. The proposal is intended to reduce congestion and produce new toll lanes without the need for any additional state funds because private companies would pay for the construction costs in return for keeping the toll revenue stream.

Virginia. Finally, the Virginia Department of Transportation has received unsolicited private sector proposals to widen the Capital Beltway from Springfield to Tysons Corner, and to widen the High Occupancy Vehicle (HOV) lanes on I-95 south of the Beltway.

As I said, this is a familiar pattern in other countries. Italy, for example, privatized its largest state toll business, Autostrade, a few years ago. In Canada, a toll road near Toronto—the 407—was privatized after being constructed by the Province of Ontario. Japan also has committed to privatizing its government-owned toll facilities, which are the largest toll revenue generators in the world. Most new toll facilities under construction around the world, in fact, are being built by investors under government-administered concessions. These include new toll roads in 23 countries in Europe, Asia, South America, and the Caribbean.

Government must rise to the challenge
It is time to ask what the federal government can do to help accelerate this trend and ensure that we maximize the benefits of private sector participation in our transportation system. Quite frankly, one of the most critical things the federal government can do simply is to get out of the way. The Administration's surface reauthorization proposal—called the Safe,

Accountable, Flexible and Efficient Transportation Equity Act, or SAFETEA—takes some important first steps toward accomplishing that goal.[1]

For example, SAFETEA would allow all states to use tolling on any highway, including interstates, so long as the aim is to reduce congestion. Road pricing is a proven congestion buster, and the time has come to allow all states to experiment in this area, not just the 15 that happened to be participants in the Federal Highway Administration's pricing pilot program. Priced lanes can give drivers a choice they don't currently have when they need a quicker, less congested route for driving to work, home, or the day care center.[2]

> Road pricing is a proven congestion buster, and the time has come to allow all states to experiment in this area.

Our proposal for private activity bonds would change federal tax rules that now strongly discourage the world's most vibrant private sector from investing in surface transportation facilities that benefit the public. SAFETEA proposes allowing state and local governments to turn over bond proceeds from a tax-exempt issuance to private entities willing to construct highways or intermodal freight facilities. This prohibition has long been cited as a primary reason the United States lags behind the rest of the world when it comes to attracting large amounts of private capital to transportation infrastructure. The private sector can bring innovation, greater efficiency and cost savings to the table, resulting in transportation projects that are completed faster and at less expense to taxpayers.[3]

Finally, our bill also has provisions that encourage greater use of private infrastructure financing by enhancing the effectiveness of State Infrastructure Banks, expanding eligibility for the Transportation Infrastructure Finance's innovative financing program, and emphasizing greater use of public-private partnerships.[4]

As Secretary of Transportation Norman Mineta often points out, while spending levels are a critical part of any reauthorization proposal—and money has been the subject of endless debate in relation to this piece of legislation—federal investments must go hand-in-hand with sound policies in order to attract new resources. Passage of SAFETEA will allow us to start thinking seriously about the more far-reaching policy changes that we will have to look at in the future.[5]

This can be done in the context of defining the federal role more broadly in terms of financing infrastructure for all modes of transportation. While that is a debate for another day, it should be clear that government should not shut out private sector investment at a time when it holds the promise of a far more robust and dynamic transportation system in the future.

1. Editor's Note: The Safe, Accountable, Flexible and Efficient Transportation Equity Act—A Legacy for Users, P. L. 109-59 ("SAFETEA-LU"), was signed into law by President Bush on August 10, 2005. The legislation as enacted contained many of the innovative provisions proposed by the Bush Administration and discussed by Mr. Shane in the speech from which this essay is excerpted.

2. Editor's Note: Although SAFETEA-LU did not authorize the tolling of any existing interstate highway segment as proposed by the Bush Administration, it did broaden the flexibility available to states in using tolling as a way to finance capacity expansion. The legislation also continues the existing 15-state pricing pilot program and added a second pilot program.

3. Editor's Note: Congress adopted the Bush Administration's proposal in SAFETEA-LU and authorized the use of private activity bonds for the financing of highway and intermodal facilities.

4. Editor's Note: Congress, in enacting SAFETEA-LU, broadly accepted the Bush Administration's proposals to expand the use of innovative financing techniques.

5. Editor's Note: The preceding section is excerpted from remarks before the Transportation Research Forum (46th Annual Forum), Washington, D.C., March 7, 2005.

Under the leadership of Secretary Mineta, our Department has also developed a new "Freight Action Agenda" to help guide our partners, our stakeholders, and ourselves in efforts to improve goods movement throughout our transportation system. The Freight Action Agenda lays out a vision that reaches far beyond where our Department has gone in the past, recognizing that freight policy, given its inherently inter-modal nature, must be driven by strong leadership.

Our agenda includes initiatives to develop better freight data and analytical tools, improve inter-modal freight research and technology, educate the next generation of freight professionals, and advance nationally significant freight projects.

We are focusing currently on three nationally significant freight Gateway projects—in Chicago, at the large port complex at Los Angeles and Long Beach, and in Seattle—because rapidly increasing demands on the system are creating serious bottlenecks in these high-demand areas. If we fail to alleviate congestion in those particular areas, businesses' track record of success will be jeopardized.

4.2

Conclusion

So what are our next steps? Clearly, we must find strategies that can help us better manage and finance network assets. Right after our surface transportation legislation is passed and the full-scale implementation of our long-awaited freight gateway program commences, we will have a frank discussion with our stakeholders about what a more comprehensive set of strategies would look like to ensure that in the 21st Century, transportation continues to serve as an engine of economic growth rather than being an impediment to it.

We will also develop a toolkit beyond what we currently possess. Market-based pricing and tax incentives are just two examples of the kinds of policy tools that will help us to address freight capacity.

We are all facing exactly the same kinds of issues and so we must learn from each other. The vision of a high-technology infrastructure brimming with creativity and innovation, and delivering more productivity gains, will be realized only if transportation and business leaders are prepared to join in waging a sustained fight for change.

These are remarks of Jeffrey N. Shane, Under Secretary for Policy, United States Department of Transportation, excerpted from presentations before the Transportation Research Forum (46th Annual Forum), Washington, D.C., March 7, 2005, and before the European Conference of Ministers of Transport, Moscow, Russia, May 24, 2005. With the approval of the U.S. Department of Transportation, the editor has combined portions of these presentations and removed remarks directed to the audience to enhance readability. The full text of these presentations is publicly available at http://ostpxweb.dot.gov.

About the United States Department of Transportation

The Department of Transportation was established by an act of Congress on October 15, 1966 and the Department's first official day of operation was April 1, 1967. The mission of the Department is to serve the United States by ensuring a fast, safe, efficient, accessible, and convenient transportation system that meets our vital national interests and enhances the quality of life of the American people, today and into the future.

Research

5

Intelligent transportation systems— can they cure congestion?

Dr. Joseph Sussman I J.R. East Professor of Civil and Environmental Engineering and Engineering Systems at Massachusetts Institute of Technology (MIT), U.S.

What I find most interesting is the way that technology is set to change the way transportation of all kinds actually works. Whether it is the problem of persuading buses to arrive on time, singly and not in bunches, smoothing the path of a business supply chain, or discussing how to arrive at an equitable solution to the problem of transportation pricing—especially on the roads—technology is an enabler.

Some issues, among the biggest of which is congestion, raise their heads wherever you go in the world. It is now generally agreed that you cannot just carry on building more roads. Given that, the question is how best to make existing transportation infrastructure more efficient with, of course, information and communications technology as the key change agent.

This is where Intelligent Transportation Systems (ITS) come in. ITS has been at the core of my work and research for the last 17 years and is about improving transportation systems using technology and information—all kinds of transportation systems, although I first focus here on highways.

ITS sits on two pillars: Advanced Transportation Management Systems (ATMS) and Advanced Traveler Information Systems (ATIS).

If we look at road networks, we see that ATMS benefits the whole driver population. It deals with the centralized management of a transportation network and is intended to provide a better service to everybody. We manage the transportation network better by getting real-time information about the flows on a network, making decisions about how to operate it more effectively, changing traffic lights and ramp metering rates, enabling better incident detection, and reducing what we call non-recurring (or random) congestion. Everybody benefits.

ATIS, on the other hand, directly benefits a relatively small segment of drivers: those willing to pay for information tailored to their needs. It is the provision of traveler information to those drivers, advising them how they might best route themselves around the transportation network. This tends to be a much more specialized service: information provided to individuals who are willing to pay for it. They receive better information than other drivers about how the network is operating, such as where traffic jams and accidents have occurred.

In the early years of ITS, the assumption was that these two services were antithetic—that they pulled in opposite directions. On the one hand we were trying to benefit the driving population at large; on the other we were operating systems only for the benefit of a smaller segment of the population—those willing to pay, and generally the more affluent.

> It is now generally agreed that you cannot just carry on building more roads. Given that, the question is how best to make existing transportation infrastructure more efficient.

5.1

That was found not to be true. Research suggests that the provision of information to a small segment of drivers helps everybody. If you provide information to 10 to 15 percent of the driving population, and they divert around the congestion, of course it helps them—we are selling a service so we presume there is value in it. But it turns out also to help everybody else on the roads. The other 85 percent also benefit because congestion is ameliorated for them as well. While it doesn't help them as much as those with specialized information, in simulations, average journey times fall for everybody, not just for the special drivers. Even if a small number of individuals decides to re-route or not to drive, it makes a big difference to traffic flows.

Public transportation and leadership

ITS can benefit public transportation operators—both bus and rail—as well as individual drivers. For example, the ability to sense vehicle locations in realtime and provide traveler information is as much, if not more, suited to public transportation as it is to drivers. We are all familiar with the bus convoy phenomenon, where you sit waiting for a bus for 20 minutes and then three arrive at once. With automatic vehicle location technology, operators could adjust bus headways and enhance both the productivity of the bus fleet *and* the quality of their service to bus users.

Long before I became involved with ITS, I studied the operating practices of freight railroads, focused on rail customers' needs, and the impact of service reliability on supply chains. Reliability relates to the variation in the trip time for a shipment between an origin and destination; often this can be more important than the average trip duration. On the freight side, when variation or unreliability occurs, it has many implications for the level of inventory. Inventory is expensive. Shippers have to hedge against unreliability in transportation service by building bigger inventories so they don't run out of stock at peaks such as Christmas. This is, of course, very costly.

We have long understood this on the freight side of the transportation business, but it is more recently that we have recognized the importance of reliability on the traveler side as well. ITS can be a big help in improving traveler reliability for individual drivers, but I believe it can be especially helpful in reducing unreliability in public transportation, often cited as a major reason people may choose not to use it.

Indeed I suggest that public transportation can be a big winner in the application of ITS, but for that industry to become an active user, institutional change and education are also needed. It means developing visionaries in those organizations who can envisage the roles that technology might play.

In particular, leadership is an important component of getting things done. Some public transportation agencies have been effective in thinking about and executing new ways of doing business, of integrating technology and thinking about their users as customers. Those are usually characterized by having strong leaders, people willing to stick their necks out and take risks. In this category, in the U.S., I would include the Chicago Transit Authority, the New York Metropolitan Transportation Authority, and Bay Area Rapid Transit. These organizations have cultivated people at the helm with, I believe, vision and the leadership abilities to move the system away from its settled equilibrium in a low-technology, less customer-sensitive world.

Rationing and congestion

My work on ITS led to a focus on Regional Strategic Transportation Planning (RSTP). Put succinctly, the goal of a regional strategic transportation plan is to ensure an adequate, efficiently operated, robust, and secure transportation network that maximizes total societal benefits within a sustainable framework. It remains the case that regional planning, focused on sustainability, new technologies, and customer service can and should replace the more narrow views that too often tend to dominate.

In my view, the art of planning for transportation at a regional level has fallen behind the kinds of real-world issues that regions face. Near the top of this list is congestion, resulting from unplanned, free access to scarce resources such as highway space.

RSTP raises a number of issues—among them equity, organizational change, and security. Looking at current RSTP practice, it tends not to reflect the more global issues that are an inherent part of economic development. This includes issues such as concerns about sustainability; the appropriate balance in a region between economic growth and development, environmental protection, and issues of social equity.

Most people agree that RSTP needs to provide benefits to all strata of society. Economic growth is important—as is environmental protection—but not if those benefits are unevenly and unfairly distributed. This is, of course, an ideological issue, as many transportation issues tend to be because of the centrality of transportation systems in everyone's life. Many transportation professionals—but not myself—disqualify one of the most useful mechanisms available to regional planners, congestion pricing, on the basis that it is inequitable and therefore inappropriate. They argue that highways are a public facility and that we should not discriminate on the basis of ability to pay. Others, like myself, argue that the price mechanism applies to a variety of other sectors, so why should highway transportation be any different, especially since wise use of congestion pricing can lead to better service for many travelers, not just those willing to pay?

5.1

> Many transportation professionals—but not myself— disqualify one of the most useful mechanisms available to regional planners, congestion pricing, on the basis that it is inequitable and therefore inappropriate.

I find it ironic that the capitalist West used to criticize the old Soviet Union for its unsophisticated way of allocating capacity by queuing. If you wanted beef, you queued until the beef ran out. If it was really important to ensure you got beef because your in-laws were coming that night, you arrived very early so there would be some left when you reached the front of the queue.

We found that lack of price rationing amusing and unsophisticated. Yet every day on our nations' highways, we do exactly the same thing; we allocate capacity by queuing. Everybody waits for their turn to enter the system whether or not they are willing to pay a premium to queue-jump, because until now, no opportunity has existed to pay that premium. Congestion charging provides that mechanism.

The idea is not new. Papers by Nobel Prize-winning economist Professor William Vickery at Columbia University in the late 1950s and early 1960s form the basis of today's congestion pricing theory and practice. It concerns how you charge people for using an infrastructure-intensive facility like a highway—or an electric power network for that matter. Capacity of such facilities remains fixed until it is either upgraded or replaced, and that capacity needs to be managed. Core to that management is the notion of providing an incentive to use the facility outside peak times. You spread demand, moving people onto the shoulders of the peaks using pricing, charging them differently at different times of day. This can benefit a large percentage of the customers.

Until the development of today's ITS technology, Vickrey's ideas have not been feasible on highways. Electronic toll collection is probably the ITS technology with which most people are familiar. You load a transponder in your car with electronic money and, as you drive through the toll, your account is debited without your having to stop.

With modern technology, it is quite straightforward to change those prices in realtime. We now have this opportunity to spread the peaks and give people a sense of choice: do you want to pay a premium to drive when you want, or are you willing to drive off-peak and be charged little or even nothing?

Probably the best example in the U.S. is the High Occupancy Toll (HOT) lanes, derived from the concept of the more familiar High Occupancy Vehicle (HOV) lanes. The public policy aim of HOV is to provide an incentive to car-pool, reducing the number of vehicles on the road by allowing car-poolers to travel in the less congested lane and therefore receive a better level of service— a faster and more reliable trip.

HOT lanes take that one step further. Enabled by ITS technologies, you can use HOV lanes when driving alone, provided you value your time enough to pay for the privilege of traveling faster. The toll can vary over time as we have seen, so off-peak, it could well be close to free. But of course at off-peak times drivers would have little motivation to use HOT lanes since the free lanes would usually be uncongested

Ultimately, though, such schemes live or die on political rather than value grounds. As I tell my students, when dealing with complex socio-technical systems like transportation, there clearly is no right answer. However, research shows that, if properly designed, by moving some people into the HOT lane, you get lower congestion in other lanes. From a pure transportation point of view, most travelers can benefit.

Change and technology

In addition to equity and sustainability, the issue of effectively integrating the systems and technologies used by the various interested parties is of vital importance. What they ultimately call for is organizational and institutional change within those transportation enterprises. By institutional change, I refer to interconnections between organizations and how institutions provide transportation services as a group at a regional scale.

Take surface transportation—highways and public transportation—for instance. For a long time it has been a very conservative and relatively low-technology business. The process of building, choice of materials, road design—all these are old ideas and not areas where technology is fast-advancing. But now, new technologies such as ITS can be employed. This involves the use of information, communication, and sensing technologies, plus advanced mathematical algorithms to manage transportation networks, in order to provide information. Organizations like state departments of transportation, which typically made advances through much more conventional kinds of technology, are undergoing a form of high-tech revolution. It implies substantial internal changes to the way in which they operate.

> Today's technology is the enabler for transportation management to be handled effectively at a regional rather than urban level. It allows decisions to be based on sound data.

But technology is only part of the story. Those organizations also need a whole new set of individuals with new kinds of talents, unlike those they have traditionally called upon. It suggests a need for reeducation of current professionals and for an infusion of bright young people from institutions of higher learning to drive the sector forward.

5.1

Think local, plan regionally

Transportation authorities need to be thinking about the new capabilities that technology brings. Although there are huge challenges—political as well as financial—examples do exist where regional bodies have made a real difference.

Today's technology is the enabler for transportation management to be handled effectively at a regional rather than urban level. It allows decisions to be based on sound data and enables the system to operate on both day-to-day and strategic bases. This ties in with the way technology is driving economic changes in the wider world. We may have a global economy but the competition that exists within that global economy is, economists tell us, increasingly taking place on a metropolitan-based, regional scale. As well as being a significant economic geographical unit, the region is also important environmentally.

Theory and practice, however, are often very different. Simply possessing the opportunity and the technology to manage systems regionally means different things to different people, depending on their point of view. For example, managing traffic flows is important to the individuals and organizations performing the management tasks, and to those whose journeys are eased as a result. But those people, through whose local streets the re-routed traffic flows, may well have a very different view of the matter.

That said, two areas where regional planning and execution have been handled well stand out. The London metropolitan area in the U.K. has made very important advances in thinking about transportation activities at a regional level. All eyes are on London's congestion charge, which has brought about very welcome relief from traffic congestion in the commercial district of the city. It has also gone hand-in-hand with increasing investment in public transportation without any apparently deleterious effects on economic activity, something many were worried about.

> All eyes are on London's congestion charge, which has brought about very welcome relief from traffic congestion in the commercial district of the city. It has also gone hand-in-hand with increasing investment in public transportation.

Similarly—and this may surprise some—the New York City metropolitan area has also made some considerable advancements. It is the most densely settled and populated region in the U.S., and if there is a region with institutional issues, it is the New York City metropolitan area. It includes three states—New York, New Jersey, and Connecticut—together with many very powerful, large-scale organizations. These include the Port Authority of New York and New Jersey, which manages infrastructure such as bridges and tunnels, and the Metropolitan Transportation Authority, which runs New York's subways and buses. Despite competing sets of interests and political jurisdictions with large fiefdoms jealous of their own prerogatives, they have seen the value of coordinating transportation across state lines and acted upon it.

It came about because of a regionally oriented organization, Transcom, initially a spin-off from the Port Authority of New York and New Jersey, which coordinates the transportation enterprise regionally both through political interactions with some 16 member organizations and by using the very latest technology. It is a good example of how new technology can enable positive institutional change.

Security and safety

Safety has always been high on the priority list for transportation planners but, since 9/11, a perceived need for strengthened security has added another dimension. Since that date, most money spent on transportation security goes towards securing us in the air. However, many transportation specialists have noted that there is huge potential for massive harm on urban public transportation systems. Yet most of those systems have either not been hardened at all, or, have been improved very modestly, compared to air transportation. With the events on London's bus system and the Underground in 2005, those weaknesses have been tragically demonstrated. We may be shocked but we should not be surprised.

When we created the concept of ITS, at the top of the agenda of proposed benefits was congestion relief. Safety was originally second but, as we thought about the numbers of deaths on U.S. roads—over 40,000 a year—it became the primary goal. That's a remarkable statistic to me—in a wealthy nation like the U.S., we lose almost the same number of people each year that we lost in the Vietnam war! A factor at play here is that human perception of risk is skewed. Small numbers of accidents that each kill a large number of people always get more attention than the large number of accidents that individually kill few but which, over time, kill one or more orders of magnitude more in total.

The emphasis in the ITS program on safety was not just because of the moral imperative, although that, of course, exists. There is also the political consideration because, in order to get political attention, you need a universal issue, one that all politicians can relate to, no matter what their local conditions. For senators from sparsely populated states like Wyoming, congestion simply is not an issue. But highway safety is a key issue. This is where in-vehicle technologies—such as technologies to improve driver alertness—come into play, because single-vehicle, run-off-the-road accidents are prevalent in rural areas.

5.1

Can we predict the future?

Predicting the future is always exciting, but to predict accurately is incredibly hard—even projecting 10 to 15 years ahead is fraught with difficulties. I believe ITS will continue to play a major part in surface transportation but, looking back on predictions made in 1991, we see that deviation from the original plan has been substantial.

But having said that, I believe it is important that organizations, institutions, and politicians begin to think on a metropolitan or regional scale, where there is enormous potential to make transportation both more efficient and more effective. Technology is a piece of that; it is important for managing transportation networks, for safety enhancements, and for providing transportation information to help people navigate the systems more easily. But, as I have discussed, it is by no means the whole answer.

Many argue that technology will fundamentally change how we work, with e-commuting or working from home reducing the demand for transportation services. While substituting communication for transportation is one option, I tend to be a pessimist about how great an effect that will have on transportation demand. My intuition is that the benefits resulting from enhanced communication will simply lead to more connections, both personal and business. This in turn will drive more demand for traditional transportation. The upshot is that any diminution of demand will be severely muted. In addition, goods and commodities still need to be delivered to supermarkets and shopping centers—that is, until the Star Trek transporter arrives!

While I am not of the opinion that technology will substantially reduce the demand for travel, I can see technology increasing effectiveness and efficiency by using pricing as a mechanism for improving services and segmenting the market to make choice a real possibility. By smoothing peaks, this makes services better for everybody.

In my view, we need to see a combination of ITS technologies and changes in organizational and institutional frameworks acting as enablers for the future. If not, we will not have the viable transportation solutions needed over the next 10 or 20 years in order to continue as an economic leader in this global economy.

The opportunities stemming from new technologies are profound. The real challenges are the pressures to perform economically and to produce sustainable transportation, balancing economic development with environmental issues and equity concerns. It will take very insightful individuals and strong leadership to grasp those opportunities throughout the world.

But it's a challenge that I welcome. I see more and more people recognizing that a partnership between the research and academic communities and the practicing profession could be marvelously efficient. Together they can look at some of these challenges—sustainability, supply chain management, and technology—and move us towards constructive change.

About the Massachusetts Institute of Technology
The mission of MIT is to advance knowledge and educate students in science, technology, and other areas of scholarship that will best serve the nation and the world in the 21st century.

The Institute admitted its first students in 1865. Today MIT is a world-class educational institution. Teaching and research—with relevance to the practical world as a guiding principle—continue to be its primary purpose.

5.1

Innovation and the transportation enterprise

Dr. Richard John | Senior Technical Advisor, John A. Volpe National Transportation Systems Center, U.S. Department of Transport, U.S.

The process of transforming the nation's transportation system in order to meet the challenges of the 21st century involves consideration of both: 1) economic, political, institutional, cultural, technological, and managerial issues, and 2) the resolution of disputes among transportation stakeholders with different concerns and priorities.

In any discussion of how best to bring about transformation and innovation in a major enterprise, it is important to note that while technology can play a significant role, it is only one component in a very complex process. There is no technological silver bullet that will solve our projected surface transport or air transportation system challenges.

The air transportation enterprise, involves many individuals and organizations: executives and employee unions; pilots and air traffic controllers; passengers and shippers; local, state, and federal governments; regulators; air carriers; the military; and general aviation. Each of these entities has a very different perspective on whether projected transformations and innovations are to their advantage or disadvantage. There are always perceived winners and losers.

How is a homeowner, located near an airport, to be compensated when his or her home is taken by eminent domain to make space for a new runway?

> The major challenge to be met by the future air transportation system is to achieve a balance between the often-competing goals of its many stakeholders and society as a whole.

How can an air traffic controller be reassured that automation won't make him or her redundant or compromise safety?

Change offers the potential to improve the situation, but it also creates uncertainty and unforeseen consequences. Change will be resisted if it appears that some organizations are "winning" at the expense of others.

Failure to give both technological and non-technological issues equal weight and priority in assessing and implementing solutions will almost always guarantee failure in any effort to bring about significant transformation and

innovation in the air transportation system, the global transportation system, or indeed any major enterprise.

The challenges

The major challenge to be met by the future air transportation system is to achieve a balance between the often-competing goals of its many stakeholders and society as a whole. In the face of an ever-expanding global economy, the need for system growth, accessibility, and affordability must be balanced against the equally important requirements for safety, security, environmental compatibility, and energy conservation.

5.2

System growth—accessibility

Today, in the most densely populated areas of the United States, the air transportation system is barely keeping pace with demand. The Federal Aviation Administration (FAA) is predicting that more than 25 major and regional airports will need additional capacity by 2025. As the carriers' business models evolve and point-to-point service is introduced using regional jets, the number of flights is growing even faster than the increase in passenger demand. This situation will be further exacerbated if there is the massive introduction of air taxis and small personal jets predicted by some observers. For example, a shift of only 2 percent of today's passengers to small (four to six passengers) jets would result in triple the number of flights in order to carry the same number of passengers

Affordability and economics

Currently, as the result of competitive market forces, passenger ticket prices for air transportation are falling and the major carriers are in dire financial condition. Some nonprofitable routes to smaller communities are being shut down, leaving segments of the population without air service. At the same time, with the reduction in ticket prices, the funds flowing into the Airport/Airway Trust Fund, which are primarily based on a percentage of the ticket price (for example 7.5 percent), are falling. Correspondingly, the funds available for operating and upgrading the air traffic management system are in short supply. The financial situation for the major air carriers and the FAA's traffic control and management system has nearly reached crisis proportions, and the implications for air passengers and shippers are not clear.

Safety

In parallel with the anticipated growth in passenger and cargo movement by air, the U.S. has the goal of further enhancing safety and maintaining aviation's record as the safest form of transportation. Safe acceleration of transformational change will require not only technological and operational innovations but also a comprehensive risk management approach based on sophisticated safety modeling and analysis.

Security

Current actions to enhance aviation security cost more than US$4 billion per year. The challenge is to find ways to improve aviation security and at the same time balance the security needs against the requirements for air system availability and speed. How can passengers be moved through an airport with minimum disruption to their travel plans, and without at the same time putting the nation at risk? As more regional and local airports are expanded across the country for use by air taxis and small business and private jets, a particularly challenging problem will be that of allocating the costs for ensuring security at facilities with low traffic volumes.

Environment

As the demand for aviation services grows, improved environmental protection will be a critical element in determining the quality and viability of the U.S. air transportation system. Looking ahead, environmental compatibility will be achieved though a combination of improvements in air traffic performance and operational procedures, restricted land use around airports, incentives for technology introduction, and aircraft de-icing procedures. If the issue is not appropriately addressed, noise and emissions will limit the capacity of major airports. The challenge is again to find a balance between environmental impact and other goals. Operational procedures aimed at limiting environmental impacts might involve trade-offs with system capacity and, in extreme cases, with system safety.

Impediments to air system transformation

There is universal agreement that the U.S. aviation system must transform itself to be more responsive to the tremendous social, economic, political, and economic changes that are sweeping the planet. As people in the developing world see their disposable incomes rise, with a concomitant rise in opportunities for leisure travel, how will the U.S. compare with other nations when it comes to attracting tourist dollars? The free and unimpeded flow of goods and people within the United States and between the United States and other countries is essential if we are to remain a leader in the global economy. The current and projected increase to the density of air traffic is making the air system increasingly inefficient. Business as usual will not succeed. The air system must be transformed.

Looking at a 25-year time horizon, nearly all projected operational concepts have similar requirements. These include:

• More runways on which aircraft can take off and land.

• More automation and computer-based decision support tools to enhance system productivity in terms of the number of aircraft that can be handled by a single controller.

• More effective use of runways and terminal airspace.

• More alignment of what the aircraft operator pays with the cost of providing the service.

The introduction of new technology is, in most cases, necessary but certainly not the limiting factor in meeting the projected requirements.

There is universal agreement that the U.S. aviation system must transform itself to be more responsive to the tremendous social, economic, political, and economic changes that are sweeping the planet.

5.2

Expanded or new airports and runways

If we are to meet the projected increase in aircraft takeoffs and landings associated with passenger and cargo movement, changing air carrier business models involving more point-to-point service, and the anticipated growth in use of small air taxis, business, and personal jets, it will be necessary to increase the operational capacity of existing and new airports through the application of new technology and by pouring more concrete. The use of new technology to tighten up aircraft separations and to obtain more effective sequencing of large and small aircraft can increase the operational capacity of a specific airport configuration; however, the increase will be well below the projected number of future operations.

If we are to meet anticipated demand, hub, regional, and small airports will have to be expanded, new airside and landside infrastructure will have to be constructed, new funding streams will have to be established, and of equal importance—homeowners and neighborhoods, impacted by the attendant noise and air pollution, will have to be addressed. From concept to operation, the installation of a new runway at a major hub airport can take from 10 to 15 or more years and cost, in some cases, more than US$1 billion dollars. The number of constituent groups that must be brought together is at best challenging. It is interesting to note that the Central Artery in downtown Boston was built in two or three years, but it has taken nearly 20 years and more than US$15 billion, from start to finish, to tear it down and replace it with a tunnel-based facility. The days of quick planning and construction for major public works are long past. Consensus building among the multitude of constituent groups impacted by the construction of a new runway or airport expansion must be considered at the beginning, not at the end of the planning process.

Automation and decision support systems

Looking ahead, it has been proposed in some quarters that it may become technologically feasible, at least under nominal conditions, to replace pilots and/or air traffic controllers with automated systems. The possibility of automation and the resultant reductions in labor requirements are initially attractive, but at what cost?

- What would be the role of the human as an operator or a manager?
- How would authority and responsibility be allocated for intervention and modification of computer-based decisions, especially under time pressure of system failure or security externalities?
- How would human operators or system managers be trained for their jobs?
- How would automated traffic systems be certified?
- How would liability be assigned and would there be a cap on liability?
- Who pays for the aircraft equipage required for operation in controlled airspace?

The use of automation and computer-based decision support tools should not be introduced with the goal of replacing humans with machines.

The use of automation and computer-based decision support tools should not be introduced with the goal of replacing humans with machines. Instead, this should be a partnership between humans and the computer that will result in better performance under all operating conditions than either could achieve alone. Again, if we are to bring about innovation in the way in which we manage air traffic flow, we should look at the air traffic system in its entirety, as a system of interacting technical and non-technical systems rather than as individual components.

Air system financing

There is a growing view that the aircraft operator should pay for the cost of the air traffic management services that it receives. If I fly in a small business jet from Boston Logan to Los Angeles/LAX, the number of transactions involved in handing me off from one air traffic controller to another, and in taking off and landing, is the same as if I were flying in a 747. The difference is that in a 747 aircraft, hundreds of passengers are each providing 7.5 per cent of his or her ticket price into the system. In my small jet, the only contribution I make is through a fuel tax. The time is fast approaching when we will have to address the highly sensitive issue as to how we can best define, allocate, and finance current and projected air traffic control and management costs in response to market forces.

Similarly, in many regions and locations around the country there is finite airport capacity for airplanes to take off and land. Although some airports are operating well below their capacity, many are facing congestion and even problems of gridlock. In the future it is going to be increasingly difficult for popular airports such as O'Hare in Chicago and LaGuardia in New York to meet passenger demand. The questions again arise:

- Will it be possible to allocate finite airport capacity in response to market forces rather than on a first-come, first-served basis?
- Should aircraft carrying more passengers and cargo get priority in the system?
- How, accordingly, can we introduce a market-based system where people will pay more if they want to fly out of an airport at a certain time of day?
- As in the situations cited previously, where and how can we find the organizational and political support to make the required changes?

5.2

In a pay-for service system, it is likely that general aviation, air taxis, and business jets will have to pay more than they do at present for air traffic management services. Small communities may require considerable subsidization to meet limited but significant demand. Obtaining a consensus on these and similar issues must involve the holistic assessment of the air transportation system as an interacting system of systems and not from the viewpoint of individual components.

Concluding thoughts

Value-based innovation within the transportation enterprise, or indeed any enterprise, involves the transformation of knowledge into new products, processes, and services to serve the customer and the public more effectively. Innovation for the sake of innovation makes little sense. My basic premise is that innovation involves financial, operational, and institutional as well as technical factors. Technology, while often involved, is seldom the controlling catalyst. The real foundation and only guarantee of continuing innovation is people.

As Lewis Branscomb, Professor Emeritus, John F. Kennedy School of Government, Harvard University and others pointed out many years ago, the pipeline or linear model of innovation, which assumes that innovations arise in the research laboratory and transition on to development, design, production, and marketing, is not applicable in the current era. Most commercial applications (and value-added innovations) are driven by market opportunities, not by scientific discovery.

The changing concepts for effective transportation decision-making include movement from:

- Exclusive to inclusive participation: all constituents are involved from the beginning of the planning process.
- Single to multiple goals: gains in system capacity must be balanced against issues of safety, security, and environmental compliance.
- Winner-takes-all to shared gains: one side cannot be seen as winning the war.
- Authoritarian to facilitating leadership: purpose of the planning process is not to deliver a complete plan but to provide useful information to all decision makers.

The major transformations of the transportation enterprise, required to meet the challenges of the 21st century global economy, require a holistic planning and implementation approach involving all the constituent stakeholders and groups whose lives will be affected.

Note: There is a growing amount of literature, including books, articles, symposia, and workshops, on the subject of enabling transformation and innovation within major government and commercial enterprises. Two reports may be of value to the reader. These are:

Securing the Future of U.S. Air Transportation—A System in Peril,
National Research Council of the National Academies, 2003; and
Integrated National Plan for the Next Generation Air Transportation System,
U.S. Department of Transportation, December 12, 2004.

About The Volpe Center
The Volpe Center has been part of the U.S. Department of Transportation (DOT) for 35 years and reports to the department's newly formed Research and Innovative Technology Administration (RITA).

RITA was established by DOT Secretary Norman Y. Mineta to more effectively coordinate and manage the U.S. DOT's research portfolio and to expedite the implementation of cross-modal technologies.

Cisco Systems

The following team of people from the Cisco Systems Internet Business Solutions Group (IBSG) have been involved in the conception of Connected Transportation and provided valuable industry insights and ideas for the publication.

Pravin Raj | Editor

DIRECTOR,
GLOBAL TRANSPORTATION LEAD,
CISCO SYSTEMS IBSG

Pravin Raj is the Director and Global Transportation Lead for the Cisco Internet Business Solutions Group. In this capacity, he serves as the industry lead within Cisco responsible for customer partnerships with leading transportation companies and for developing Cisco's Point-of-View for this industry. His customer advisory work at Cisco has focused on being a catalyst for change while consulting with global companies on enterprise productivity, business growth, and transformation through the improved use of information technology.

Customers in the Global Transportation Practice include large global airlines, major cargo/logistics providers, railroads, airports, seaports, and mass transit agencies.

Prior to joining Cisco, Pravin was Senior Manager for Ernst & Young LLP and Director for American Airlines Decision Technologies. Pravin has led or participated in business strategy, systems design, and implementation and large program management assignments across multiple industries and geographies.

Pravin Raj has a Bachelor's degree in Mechanical Engineering and a Masters degree in Industrial Engineering and Operations Research.

Syed Hoda | Editor
DIRECTOR, RETAIL AND TRANSPORTATION,
CISCO SYSTEMS IBSG

Syed Hoda is a Director in the Retail and Transportation Practice for the Cisco Internet Business Solutions Group. IBSG's mission is to help customers transform their organizations by strategically applying process innovation and technology to drive business results.

Prior to Cisco, Syed worked for Cap Gemini Ernst & Young, where his areas of focus included brand/marketing strategy and consumer buying behavior. He also helped develop CGE&Y's thought leadership in the consumer space, including "Consumer Relevancy"—a methodology to assess a brand's position relative to competitors. This methodology was the basis for a published book titled, *The Myth of Excellence*.

Prior to Ernst & Young, he worked for Kurt Salmon Associates, a global management consulting firm specializing in the retail and consumer products industries. His areas of focus included business strategy, supply chain management, and IT strategy with clients throughout North America, Europe, and Japan.

Syed holds a Masters degree in International Business from Emory University (Atlanta, GA) and a degree in Industrial Engineering at Case Western University (Cleveland, OH).

Howard Lock | Editor
SENIOR EXECUTIVE ADVISOR, TRANSPORTATION,
CISCO SYSTEMS IBSG

A veteran of the transportation industry, Howard has over 20 years of broad-based experience in this industry. Prior to joining the Cisco Internet Business Solutions Group, Howard headed the transportation practice for Marconi Telecommunications—a global supplier of telecommunications and information technology equipment and services. In this capacity, he had direct responsibility for strategy, marketing, and business development, including development of innovative technology solutions for the Americas region.

Prior to Marconi, Howard was with ARINC Inc., a globally recognized provider of telecommunications services, IT products, and system integration services to the global transportation community. At ARINC, he served in a variety of roles, the last of which was creating and leading ARINC's global air transportation business development group.

Howard Lock is a graduate of the U.S. Naval Academy (BS ME) and George Washington University (MS IT) and has served as a pilot in the U.S. Navy.

Gerald T. Charles, Jr., | Editor

DIRECTOR, PUBLIC SECTOR,
CISCO SYSTEMS IBSG

Gerald Charles is a Director in the Public Sector Practice of the Cisco Internet Business Solutions Group. His areas of expertise involve the Internet, security, communications, transactional processing, e-Business, and ERP applications. Gerald has developed and implemented mergers & acquisitions as well as strategic, operational, and financial goals.

Prior to Cisco, he was Vice President for OAO Technology Solutions (OAOT), where he implemented an IT solution provider practice and started the company's Public Sector Division. Before OAOT, he was a Vice President for TRW and BDM, where he brought in multimillion dollar contracts and was a key technical and program architect for implementation of U.S. Securities and Exchange Commission's EDGAR system.

As a Thought Leader, he is the author of *The LAN Blueprint: Engineering It Right*, (McGraw-Hill). Charles has also earned a Congressional Medal for Outstanding Service and Achievement.

Gerald Charles holds an M.Sc. in Electrical Engineering from the University of Maryland and a B.Sc. in Electrical Engineering from the Illinois Institute of Technology.

Dr. Amir Fattah | Editor

SENIOR EXECUTIVE ADVISOR,
CISCO SYSTEMS IBSG

Dr. Amir Fattah works for Cisco Systems IBSG as Senior Executive Advisor in Germany for world-leading companies, leveraging over 13 years of broad-based international business experience in the high-tech, telecommunications, transportation, and energy & utilities industries.

He was the Managing Director of a company in the service industry for several years and spent many years in top management consulting with Roland Berger and Accenture, where he was a member of the German management team.

During his consulting work he helped companies build new business, restructure their businesses, develop strategies and business models, design processes, to spin-off, to conduct due-diligence, and to go through mergers & acquisition. Additionally he has been advisor of a venture backed telecommunications company in Germany.

He attained his Diploma in Computer Science and Economics from Technische Universität Munich, Germany and a Ph.D. in Business Administration from the University of St. Gallen in Switzerland.

Val Stoyanov | Editor

DIRECTOR, IBSG,
CISCO SYSTEMS IBSG

Val Stoyanov has devoted his career to helping executives in the public and private sectors globally succeed with their business driven technology initiatives. In the past several years, his client advisory work has focused in on visioning, strategy, transformation, governance, innovation, and advanced solutions.

At Cisco, Val Stoyanov has helped major organizations in Public Sector, Retail, Transportation, Manufacturing and Financial Services identify economic opportunities in excess of U.S. $1 billion through deployment of networked processes and solutions.

Prior to joining Cisco in 1999, Val Stoyanov held leadership positions at high-tech companies such as Hewlett-Packard and Apple Computer. His diverse background, global experience and broad solutions expertise, enables him to effectively take customers from opportunity identification to benefits realization.

Val Stoyanov has a M.Sc. in Electrical Engineering and is a high-tech industry veteran, with 20 years of leadership experience in engineering, sales, business development, strategic partnering and consulting.

Authors

Dr. Frank Appel
CEO, DHL LOGISTICS AND MANAGEMENT BOARD MEMBER,
DEUTSCHE POST AG,
GERMANY

Dr Frank Appel holds a MSc in Chemistry from the University of Munich and a PhD in Neurobiology, from the Swiss Federal Institute of Technology in Zurich.

In 1993 he was appointed consultant and project manager at McKinsey's Frankfurt office and was elected to Partner in 1999. In 2000 he accepted the post of Managing Director, Corporate Development, at Deutsche Post AG and joined the Board in 2002.

John Belcher
CHAIRMAN AND CEO,
ARINC INC.,
U.S.

John Belcher joined ARINC in 1997 as President and Chief Operating Officer, and in 2002 was appointed Chief Executive Officer. He was also named Chairman in 2004.

Belcher has more than 30 years' experience in the aviation, information technology, and defense industries. Previous executive positions he has held include: President and CEO, Hughes Aircraft of Canada, Ltd; Vice President, Hughes Aircraft Company; President and CEO, Thompson-Hickling Aviation; Senior Vice President, PRIOR Data Sciences; Executive Director, Transport Canada, and Director General, Supply and Services Canada.

A leading authority in aviation and air traffic services, John Belcher served as Chairman of the Canadian Advanced Technology Association and on the Board of Directors for numerous trade associations and aerospace technology companies.

Bill DeCota
DIRECTOR OF AVIATION,
THE PORT AUTHORITY OF NEW YORK AND NEW JERSEY,
U.S.

Bill DeCota joined The Port Authority of New York and New Jersey as a financial analyst in 1982 and quickly rose through the ranks, serving as Manager of the Aviation Department's Business and Financial Services Division, Assistant Director of Aviation for Business and Properties and Deputy Director of Aviation.

He holds a bachelor's degree from the University of Mississippi and an MBA from the University of Georgia. The author of numerous papers on international airport planning, airport finance, and related topics, he is a member of the Policy Review Committee of the Board of the American Association of Airport Executives and former Chairman of the Finance and Administration Subcommittee of the Airports Council International.

Pierre Graff
PRESIDENT AND CEO,
AÉROPORTS DE PARIS,
FRANCE

Pierre Graff was appointed Chairman and Chief Executive Officer of Aéroports de Paris on 27 July 2005.

After several engineering positions at Regional Development and Equipment Directorates, he became, in 1986, Technical Advisor in charge of the roads policy at the Cabinet of the Ministry of Equipment, Housing, Planning and Transports, then Inter-ministerial Delegate for Road Safety from 1987 to 1990. Until 1993, he was Regional Director of the Equipment and then became Deputy Cabinet Director and Director at the Ministry of Equipment, Transport and Tourism.

From 1995 to 2002, he was General Director of the French Civil Aviation and served as Cabinet Director to Gilles de Robien, Minister of Equipment, Transport, Housing, Tourism, and the Sea from June 2002 to September 2003, before being appointed Chairman of Aéroports de Paris

Pierre Graff is a member of the Economic and Social Council and a member of the RATP Board of Administration. He is also an Officer of the French Legion of Honour.

Sir Rod Eddington
FORMER CEO,
BRITISH AIRWAYS,
UK

Sir Rod Eddington was educated at the University of Western Australia and Oxford University (the 1974 Rhodes Scholar from Western Australia).

He completed a DPhil in the Department of Engineering Science at Oxford and then taught as research lecturer at Pembroke College Oxford in 1978–79. In 1979 he joined the Swire Group and worked with Cathay Pacific Airways in Hong Kong, Korea, and Japan in a variety of roles, before being appointed Managing Director in early 1992.

He left the Swire Group at the end of 1996 to return to Australia. In January 1997 News Ltd appointed him as Executive Chairman of Ansett Airlines in Melbourne. He held that post until April 2000 when News Ltd sold its 50 percent share in Ansett. He remains on the Boards of News Corp and John Swire & Sons Pty Ltd.

Eddington was appointed Chief Executive of British Airways in 2000. Still at BA at the time this essay was written, he retired in September 2005.

August Wilhelm Henningsen

CEO AND CHAIRMAN OF THE EXECUTIVE BOARD,
LUFTHANSA TECHNIK,
GERMANY

August Wilhelm Henningsen has been Chairman of the Executive Board of Lufthansa Technik since January 2001. Henningsen joined Lufthansa German Airlines in 1979 after graduating from Brunswick Technical University.

He subsequently took charge of the company's flight control group, before being promoted to Manager of Aircraft Structure and Systems Engineering. In 1989, he was appointed Head of the department responsible for aircraft cabins and systems, and two years later took charge of the company's Boeing 737 airframe overhaul business unit.

From November 1993 until May 1997, Henningsen headed the aircraft components services division at Lufthansa Technik. He subsequently became General Manager of AMECO (Aircraft Maintenance and Engineering Corporation) in Beijing, a joint venture between Deutsche Lufthansa and Air China. On April 1, 2000 Mr Henningsen moved back to Germany as a member of Lufthansa Technik's Executive Board in charge of products and services.

Dr. Richard John

SENIOR TECHNICAL ADVISOR,
JOHN A. VOLPE NATIONAL TRANSPORTATION SYSTEMS CENTER,
U.S. DEPARTMENT OF TRANSPORT, U.S.

Dr. Richard R. John has served as Director of the John A. Volpe National Transportation Systems Center in Cambridge, Massachusetts from 1989-2004 and is currently Senior Technical Advisor at the Center.

He is a recognized leader in promoting and strengthening transportation and technological innovation in the transportation community. Dr. John is working closely with the National Aeronautics and Space Administration and the Federal Aviation Administration to transform the nation's air transport system.

François Lamoureux

DIRECTOR-GENERAL,
TRANSPORTATION AND ENERGY DIRECTORATE,
EUROPEAN COMMISSION, BELGIUM

François Lamoureux has worked at the European Commission (EC) since 1978 and has been Director-General of the Transportation and Energy Directorate since 2000. In 1996, he accepted the post of Deputy Director-General, responsible for relations with Europe and the New Independent States. In 1995 he was Chef de Cabinet at the Office of the Commissioner for Research, Education and Training, while from 1993 to 1994 he was Director of the Industry Directorate.

From 1991 to 1992, he moved to Paris, working as Deputy Director of the French Prime Minister's Office, after six years as Advisor and subsequently Deputy Chef de Cabinet at the President Jacques Delors' Office of the EC. Prior to this, he spent six years as Administrator at the Legal Service and Secretariat-General.

John Mullen

JOINT CEO, DHL EXPRESS AND MANAGEMENT BOARD MEMBER,
DEUTSCHE POST AG,
GERMANY

John Mullen is the Joint Chief Executive Officer for DHL Express, responsible for the Americas, Asia Pacific, the Middle East, and all other geographic areas outside Western Europe. He is also a member of the Board of Management of Deutsche Post World Net, the parent of DHL.

Prior to his current role, Mullen was responsible for DHL's operations in Asia Pacific and his experience has also included 10 years with the TNT Group, with two years as the Chief Operating Officer. From 1991 to 1994 he held the position of Chief Executive Officer of TNT Express Worldwide.

André Navarri
EXECUTIVE VP, BOMBARDIER INC.
AND PRESIDENT, BOMBARDIER TRANSPORTATION,
CANADA

André Navarri was appointed President of Bombardier Transportation in February 2004 and in December 2004 was appointed Executive Vice President of Bombardier Inc.

Prior to joining Bombardier, he was President of Operations at Alcatel from 1996 to 1999, where he was responsible for manufacturing operations, purchasing, business processes, information systems and quality. Navarri is also the former Chairman and Chief Executive Officer of automotive component supplier Valeo SA; he spent a large part of his career with Alstom, culminating in his appointment to President of the Transportation Division in 1996.

In May 2005, Navarri was named Chairman of the Association of the European Railway Industries (UNIFE).

David Neeleman
CHIEF EXECUTIVE OFFICER AND CHAIRMAN,
JETBLUE AIRWAYS,
U.S.

David Neeleman is Chief Executive Officer and Chairman of the board of JetBlue Airways. He has served in both capacities since August 1999.

He was a co-founder of WestJet and from 1996 to 1999 served as a member of WestJet's board of directors. From October 1995 to October 1998, Mr. Neeleman served as the Chief Executive Officer and a member of the Board of Directors of Open Skies, a company that develops and implements airline reservation systems and which was acquired by the Hewlett Packard Company.

From 1988 to 1994, Neeleman served as President and was a member of the Board of Directors of Morris Air Corporation, a low-fare airline acquired by Southwest Airlines. For a brief period, in connection with the acquisition, he served on the Executive Planning Committee at Southwest Airlines. From 1984 to 1988, Mr. Neeleman was an Executive Vice President of Morris Air.

Dr. David Pang
CEO,
AIRPORT AUTHORITY HONG KONG

Dr. David Pang was appointed Chief Executive Officer of the Airport Authority Hong Kong. in January 2001. His previous positions have included Corporate Vice President of E.I. DuPont and Vice President and General Manager of DuPont Global Nonwoven Business and Chairman of DuPont Greater China.

Dr. Pang is also President and Executive Committee Member of the Airports Council International (Pacific Region) and Board Member and Executive Committee Member of the World Governing Board of the Airports Council International, the international association of the world's airports. He is also a Council Member of Save the Children, Hong Kong.

Jeffrey N. Shane
UNDER SECRETARY FOR POLICY,
DEPARTMENT OF TRANSPORTATION,
U.S.

Jeffrey N. Shane was appointed as Under Secretary of Transportation for Policy in 2003. In this position, he serves as principal policy advisor to the Secretary of Transportation, with oversight responsibility for the Office of Transportation Policy and the Office of Aviation and International Affairs. President Bush earlier appointed Shane as Associate Deputy Secretary of Transportation, a position in which he served for a year prior to his current appointment.

Before returning to public service, Shane was a partner at the international law firm of Hogan & Hartson L.L.P. in Washington D.C. with a domestic and international transportation practice, majoring on regulatory, legislative, and transactional issues.

From 1994 through 2001 Shane was Chairman of the Commission on Air Transport of the International Chamber of Commerce and Chairman of the Military Airlift Committee of the National Defense Transportation Association. He was Chair of the American Bar Association's Forum on Air and Space Law from 2001 to early 2002. From 1985 through 1989, he was Adjunct Professor of Law at Georgetown University.

Dr. Joseph Sussman
J.R. EAST PROFESSOR OF CIVIL AND ENVIRONMENTAL
ENGINEERING AND ENGINEERING SYSTEMS, MIT,
U.S.

Dr. Sussman has served as a faculty member at MIT for 37 years. He is the author of *Introduction to Transportation Systems* and in 2005 he authored *Perspectives on Intelligent Transportation Systems*, which expands on many of the concepts discussed in his essay in this book.

Dr. Sussman specializes in planning, investment analysis, operations, management, design and maintenance of Complex, Large-Scale, Interconnected, Open Sociotechnical, Systems (CLIOS Systems), working in many applications areas. His research in railroads focuses on service reliability and rail operations, rail risk assessment in the U.S. and Japan.

Dr. Sussman has worked on Intelligent Transportation Systems (ITS), helping to build the U.S.' national program. In 2001, the ITS Massachusetts established the Joseph M. Sussman Leadership Award in recognition of his contributions to, and leadership in, ITS. Sussman received the Roy W. Crum Award from TRB, its highest honor, "for significant contributions to research" in 2001.

Chua Kee Thiam
HEAD OF INFORMATION TECHNOLOGY,
PSA SINGAPORE TERMINALS,
SINGAPORE

Chua Kee Thiam graduated with a BSc in Chemistry and Mathematics from the National University of Singapore in 1982. He joined PSA in 1982 as a Trainee Systems Analyst/Programmer and became Systems Analyst/Programmer in 1984. He was appointed Deputy Manager in June 1993 and subsequently Manager (Billing & Information Systems) in July 1997. He became the New Terminal Systems Manager in August 1998 and Corporate Services Systems Manager in November 1999. Chua Kee Thiam was re-designated E-Services and E-Business Programme Director in 2000. In September 2000, he assumed the role of Project Director (Container Systems) and was promoted to the position of Vice-President (Container Systems) in July 2001. He has held the position of Head of Information Technology since July 2004.

The Connected Series
Essays from innovators

A series of thought-provoking books covering top-of-mind issues across a range of public and private industry sectors. Each book sets out a Cisco perspective on the sector, and includes a range of essays from many of the world's leading CXOs, innovators, and visionaries.

Connected Cities
Edited by Simon Willis

The ideas explored in Connected Cities chart the emergence of a political and economic phenomenon—the city as the connected republic of the 21st Century. Simon Willis, Global Head of eGovernment for the Internet Business Solutions Group at Cisco Systems, has collated essays that show how different cities are grappling with the various stages of connectivity.

ISBN 0-9546445-1-4   160 x 240mm   116 pages

Connected Health
Edited by Kevin Dean

Healthcare is consistently debated and the highest priority on the agenda of citizens, public servants and nations. The advent of the Internet and communication technologies is changing the way we provide care. This intellectually stretching collection of essays highlights the drivers for changing the way information is used to deliver better, faster, lower cost healthcare—and describes real-world experience.

ISBN 0-9546445-0-6   160 x 240mm   116 pages

Connected Schools
Edited by Michelle Selinger

We live in a Knowledge Society, where connectivity delivers information at unprecedented speeds and in multiple formats, and creates opportunities for new partnerships. In this exciting age, education is the prime driver for economic growth, peace and prosperity. Connected Schools demonstrates how governments across the world have realized the need to focus resources on the evolution of their educational systems and have used new technology and the Internet to drive change.

ISBN 0-9546445-5-7   160 x 240mm   168 pages